Basic Training of the Young Horse

Dressage · Jumping · Cross-country

INGRID AND REINER KLIMKE

Basic Training of the Young Horse

Dressage · Jumping · Cross-country

Trafalgar Square
North Pomfret, Vermont

This third edition published in the United States of America in 2015 by
Trafalgar Square Books
North Pomfret, Vermont 05053
www.HorseandRiderBooks.com

Published simultaneously in Great Britain by J.A. Allen, London

Originally published in the German language as *Klimke, Grundausbildung des jungen Reitpferdes* by Franckh-Kosmos Verlags-GmbH & Co. KG, Stuttgart

ISBN: 978-1-57076-760-9

Library of Congress Control Number: 2015942147

Disclaimer of Liability

The authors and the publisher shall have neither liability nor responsibility to any person or entity with respect to any loss or damage caused or alleged to be caused directly or indirectly by the information contained in this book. While the book is as accurate as the authors can make it, there may be errors, omissions, and inaccuracies.

Translated by Claire Lilley
Edited by Martin Diggle

Printed in China

For my dear father

Ingrid Klimke

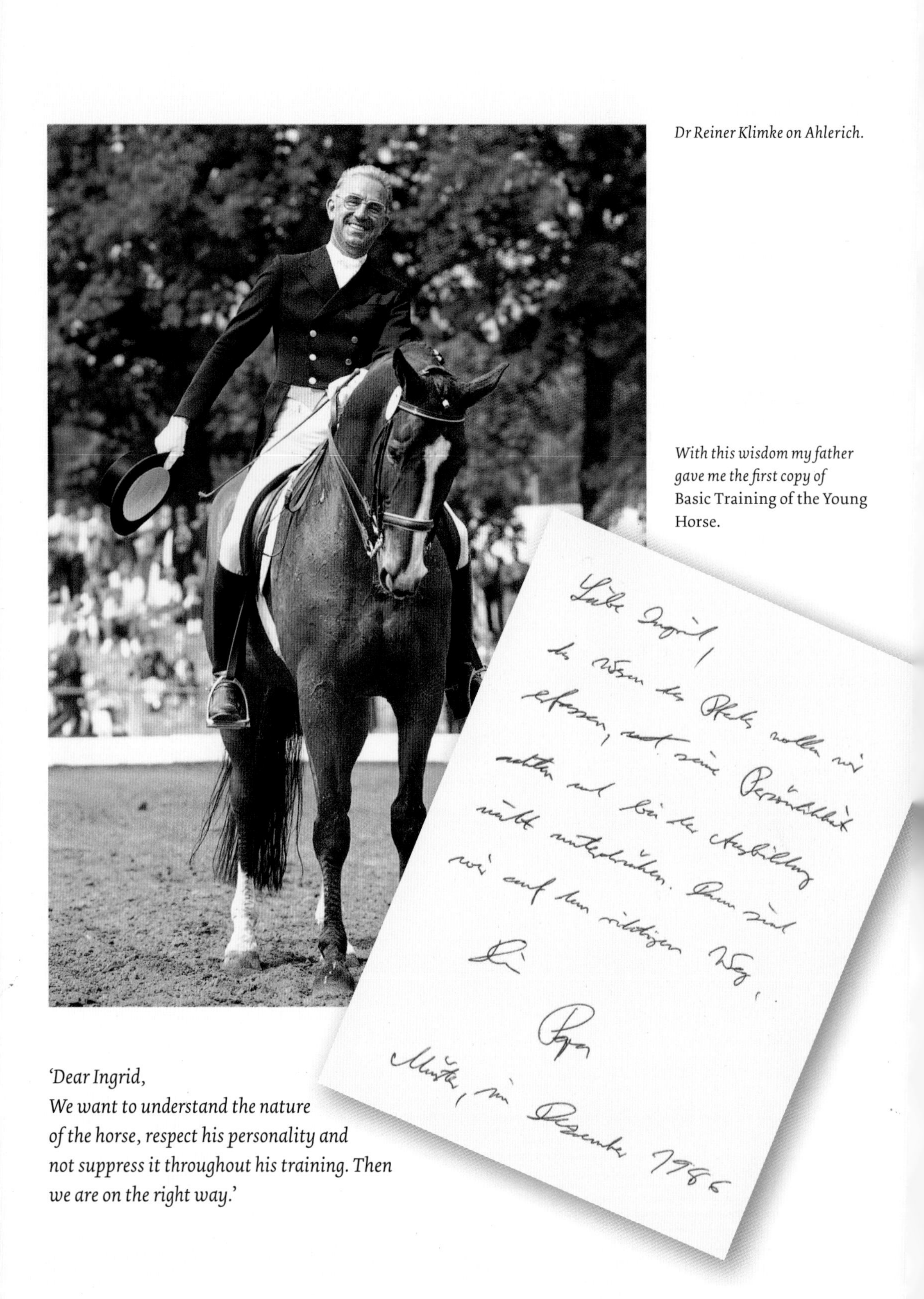

Liebe Ingrid,
das Wesen des Pferdes wollen wir erfassen, und seine Persönlichkeit achten und bei der Ausbildung nicht unterdrücken. Dann sind wir auf dem richtigen Weg.
Dein
Papa
Münster, im Dezember 1986

Dr Reiner Klimke on Ahlerich.

With this wisdom my father gave me the first copy of Basic Training of the Young Horse.

'Dear Ingrid,
We want to understand the nature of the horse, respect his personality and not suppress it throughout his training. Then we are on the right way.'

Contents

Photographic credits

183 photos were provided for this book by Horst Streitferdt/Kosmos.

Other photos by: Hanna Broms; Werner Ernst; Dominique Gautier; Roland Hogrebe; LL-Foto ; Thoms Lehmann; Fritz Ligges; Phelps Photos; Phototec; Profoto; Julia Rau / Kosmos; Julia Rau; Jan Reumann; Inge Vogel; Anne Wiegelmann; Martin Wissmann@pics2u.de.

Diagrams

With 28 diagrams by Cornelia Koller and Atelier Krohmer

Information about Ingrid Klimke
can be found on her home page: **www.klimke.org**

Preface

Remembering Dr Reiner Klimke

As one of the world's most successful riders, Dr Reiner Klimke combined rare theoretical wisdom with his practical knowledge. For many years, in addition to pursuing his professional career, he trained a number of young horses single-handed.

No other rider has self-trained so many successful horses, who went on to become champions of Germany, Europe and the World and also achieved Olympic success in the two disciplines of dressage and eventing. The idea for this book and the advice given in it was based upon this experience. With such clear proof of success and expert opinion there was no one better qualified to write about the training of young horses.

It is significant that a great authority such as Dr Klimke did not view the training of young horses only through the eyes of a dressage rider. He felt strongly that the correct understanding of basic training means the development of the horse's natural ability in all respects, whether the horse was destined for hacking, jumping or dressage. Having begun this book himself, Dr Klimke was joined in the task by his daughter, Ingrid, herself a very successful competitor in both dressage and eventing, and they worked together on the chapters on jumping and cross-country training as the book evolved. After Dr Klimke's unexpected early death, Ingrid took over the task alone, following precisely in her father's footsteps. Thus the finished book not only follows the long-established teachings of classical equitation but also contains the combined theoretical knowledge and practical experience of both Klimkes, father and daughter, thereby offering an outstanding level of guidance to the training of young horses.

Basic Training of the Young Horse should undoubtedly be recognized as a standard training book. It is easy to understand and as equally helpful and valuable for the young rider training their own horse as it is for experienced trainers and breeders. Following all the advice given from a basic level of work upwards over an appropriate timescale ensures correct and sustainable progress.

Paul Stecken, manager of the Westphalian Riding and Driving School from 1950 to 1985

Ingrid and Dr Reiner Klimke

CHAPTER 1

Basic Education

The aim of basic training

We live in a time of change. Modern technology has made everything easier and quicker; it has changed people's lives. What often took a year, now takes a fraction of the time. Speed plays a definite role in our lives but can have some unfortunate consequences where horses are concerned.

At horse auctions, 3-year-old animals have been shamefully offered for sale as top dressage horses or eventers. Horses who were only just broken to saddle were already believed to have the attributes to go far in a specific discipline. An experienced horse-handler, who knows the long, patient process needed to educate a young horse from basic training to specializing in the various disciplines, cannot countenance this. But how many horse-lovers nowadays have sufficient expertise to put this process into practice? In recent years, much of the riding fraternity has relocated from the countryside to the town. A new generation of riding enthusiasts is growing up, but they have not grown up with horses. They either view their free time with the horse as simply having contact with nature, or as a form of sport. Nowadays, too many riders are more interested in boasting about their recent purchase than in learning about stable management and the details of training the horse.

The outcome of this approach is obvious in riding competitions – how many dressage and jumping horses do you see with their necks held in tightly – horses who have not learned to find their balance in the three basic gaits and are already competing in Elementary and Medium level dressage? How many horses have never seen cavalletti or ground-poles, or do not have the opportunity to relax out hacking?

Another point is that, in many cases, degenerative bone conditions are caused by physical wear and tear and are the result of specializing in a certain discipline far too early. Over the last few years horses have been bred with better necks (with regard to conformation and how the

A 3-year-old horse working with a long neck position.

neck is set on the body), and this desirable feature should be allowed to remain so, but the young horses are ridden too quickly in the gaits too soon, and with a short rein contact. Inevitably, the looseness of the back is overlooked. A longer and deeper positioning of the neck (a lowered neck but with the forehead vertical to the ground) is essential for the development of the back as the centre of movement. This incorrect riding explains why so many horses have tight backs and restricted movement, with the possibility of sustaining back injuries which frequently require treatment by the vet. Riders also tend to sit on horses rather than riding them forwards sufficiently to be in front of the leg, resulting in tense, restricted gaits.

The aim of basic training for the young horse is to use a systematic method to create a solid foundation for future specialization in a given discipline. This development is not possible with a tight rein contact. We want the young horse, with the weight of the rider on his back, to stay in balance and outline while retaining his natural movement. This is the starting point for developing his potential for the future; in this way, basic training will be established which will enable the desired goals to be achieved with further progress. Even so, just as is the case with people, not every horse will reach top level in the chosen discipline. Many riders are happy to achieve Novice level, and are fully aware that this level of training is as far as they will get with their horses. On the other hand, there are riders who aim at a higher level

Goals of basic training

- After about one year of training the horse should be comfortable with new surroundings and used to external influences, accustomed to the stable yard, the indoor school and the dressage arena, hacking out quietly, and jumping basic courses including a variety of cross-country obstacles.
- He should have learned to understand and respond to the seat, rein and leg aids, the voice, whip and spurs.
- By this time he should have developed sufficient trust, rideability, strength and stamina to compete at Novice level dressage without any great problems, and possibly to cope with basic-level showjumping and cross-country courses safely and with a good technique.

than they or their horses are capable of achieving. They do not blame themselves, but blame their horses as they strive for more, destroying the horse's trust in the process. A correctly trained horse should have few problems at Novice level but a horse who is forced to compete before he is ready will become tense and may develop further problems in the future.

Experience acquired during the basic training of a young horse can provide valuable insight into his future training and which area to specialize in. However, experience also teaches that we should not be too dogmatic in our approach. While it is true that we give all our horses a thorough grounding in dressage, we have had many horses with a considerable talent for this discipline who have later developed as jumpers, because they were responsive to the aids, physically strong and simply enjoyed jumping. Conversely, we have had others who were very clean and careful jumpers of small fences, but fell by the wayside when the jumps got bigger, and were thus redirected in other directions.

A moment's reflection will confirm that these examples reinforce the fact that thorough basic training is important for all riding horses, whether they are destined for recreational riding or for the competitive disciplines. Careful gymnastic work aimed at muscle building and achieving suppleness of the back, and developing responsiveness to the aids, are essential in order that the horse remains healthy and is able to cope with more specialized training in the future.

Patriot

The best example of developing training is the 'pensioner' Patriot, who came to the yard as a 3-year-old. Certainly, no one saw him having a career as a dressage horse. Together, we trained him to Grand Prix and under the instruction of Fritz Ligges trained him to showjump at grade A level.

Patriot, by Palast. Trained to the top level in more than one discipline.

The handling and education of young horses

In times past, it was very common for a trainer to take on the education of a horse from a foal. During the foal's development basic rules were learned easily, making it far easier to introduce ridden work later on. Normally, nowadays, riders buy horses who are 3 or 4 years of age and already ridden. They have little knowledge about the horse's previous ownership or how a young horse should be handled in the early stages before he is ridden for the first time. By caring for a young horse one learns not only how to feed and look after him but how to develop his training in the future.

A 3-year-old horse who has been brought up as one of the family trusts people and his surroundings, so he is naturally easier to train as he becomes older, being more accustomed to civilization than he would be if he had grown up in the field. However, despite this initial advantage, we have found horses who have spent longer 'in the wild' just as good to train in the long term as those brought up as 'one of the family'. While the former are often more afraid and need more care at first, once they have learned to trust people they become very dependable.

It is extremely difficult to win the trust of young horses who have been badly started by the wrong people. They are certainly difficult during their basic training but one has to find out slowly and gently

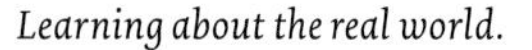

Learning about the real world.

what the previous problems were in order to overcome them. However, despite the important need to win their trust, problems can be caused when training young horses by being too gentle with them and as a consequence they make poor progress – but generally this can be put right. It is very much a personal matter for the rider, but one should not try to 'humanize' a horse.

Education begins as a foal

A good breeder establishes the basis of trust by rearing and handling young horses correctly, which prepares them for subsequent work with a rider. Education begins as a foal. The first days and weeks set the foundations for later development of a trustful working partnership between man and horse, not by hours of aimless playing around with foals, but by winning their trust. This begins with them becoming accustomed to the stable. Foals are naturally inquisitive and after a while will investigate contact with people, but they are braver more quickly if one crouches down to their level and waits until the foal comes to you. This acceptance of human contact is developed by keeping low and stroking the foal at first, progressing to holding him with the left arm under the neck and lightly passing the right arm around the hindquarters. Through this he learns that existence in the world is not entirely a matter of being free. His inborn urge for freedom must be slowly but surely brought under control.

What Hans has not learnt, young Hans will never know.

Once the foal lets you hold him for a short time a headcollar can be introduced (it must not be too big), which can be fastened around the foal's neck. The advantage of this is that you do not have to interfere with the sensitive ear area. Once it is in place, the foal must be praised. This is enough for the first lesson. When the foal accepts the headcollar confidently, then you can begin leading him.

To start with when leading, one must go along with the free movement of the foal. This can be done first of all in the stable provided it is a minimum of 15–16 square metres, such as a foaling box. The next step is to lead the mare from the stable to a nearby field with the foal following, wearing a headcollar. You need two people for this as a young mare can become unsettled by this first outing. This short walk should just be fun for the foal and a way of quickly building his

Building trust through touch.

self-confidence, so discretion is important in these first days of holding and leading the foal. Pulling at the rope can be detrimental and should be avoided. If the foal stops, the person leading the mare should walk ahead undeterred. The further the mare walks away from the foal the more inclined he will be to follow. From experience, the person leading the foal should have learned not to turn to look at him but to stand their ground and expect him to follow.

Once the foal's trust has been won and he has been led successfully he must be praised immediately. A short word of praise is enough. Excessive patting and caressing at this age are dangerous as this arouses the foal's urge to play and may encourage him to nip, which is not desirable.

Respect and trust

Respect and trust go hand in hand and are essential elements to successful training.

Foals are inquisitive. They want to smell and nibble everything such as halters, ropes, and sometimes their mother's mane and tail. Even the handler's arm will do. If you allow the foal to play around with you, you will not surprisingly be covered in bruises. Vicious biting from the foal, which is distinct from inquisitive nipping, should be recognized and punished. Maliciousness is frequently made worse by anxiety on behalf of the handler. Experienced breeders do not allow close-contact playing with the foals. They would rather keep the youngsters at a safe distance and occupied with educational exercises for a few minutes at a time.

When the foal totally accepts being led behind his mother you can begin the next stage, which is to tie him up. In times past, this was done outside using a strong rope or chain which would not break if the foal pulled at it. Later, research by vets found that the inability to co-ordinate muscular movement could be caused by strong pressure on the upper vertebrae of the neck, so this method has been superseded.

Stable manners are learnt as a foal.

Tying up must first be done in the stable. The lead-rope is passed through a ring on the wall and the end of the rope is held loosely in the hand, which enables you to give and take as necessary. Tying the foal to the mother's girth and going for a short walk is another way of introducing the idea fairly easily. The foal must learn to stand still beside his handler when the handler is still.

Grooming and picking up the feet come next. Foals love their coats being brushed gently with either a rubber curry comb or a brush. They often begin to nibble the person brushing them in return as a sign of grateful thanks. Should they bite, however, it is best to push them away or reprimand them with the voice in a sharp manner such as 'leave it!' This behaviour with people is not desirable and must be corrected before the foal grows up.

Foals learn easily to pick up their feet. One begins with the leg that has the least weight on it and lifts it, not too high, so that the foal does not lose his balance. It does not matter if a front or hind foot is picked up first, but saying 'foot' as the leg is raises teaches the foal the relevant voice command so that he understands readily what is required.

Experienced breeders are satisfied when a young foal will pick his feet up, accept being groomed and can be led around on the halter.

Getting used to leading in hand.

More than this is not required at this stage; training a horse is a long and difficult enough process without extending it any further. In the first and second year the young horse should be given the chance to grow up naturally and he should spend plenty of time out in the field.

How old should a horse be to start ridden work?

There are trainers who occasionally jump yearlings and 2-year-old horses over small fences or cavalletti. There are also trainers who lunge horses of this age. It is a mistake to do either of these too soon, knowing the problems that can arise with young horses. Warmbloods in particular can suffer from health and physical problems if they are trained too intensively in the first two years. An additional factor is that, at this age, horses grow at different rates in the front and hind parts of their bodies. Thus they are sometimes higher at the croup than at the withers, which causes difficulties with balance.

As mentioned earlier, however, it is known that, in some breeding circles, horses are produced early and ridden as 3-year-olds to be sold as 'fully trained' at the auctions. In flat racing, many horses run their first races as 2-year-olds and the season for the Derby and other Classic races is the following year. Successful racehorses are returned to stud for breeding after a very few years at the end of their racing careers.

Despite such examples of enforced precocity, the experienced, responsible trainer starts training the horse when his joints, bones and tendons are mature enough to withstand the work. Our philosophy is that no Warmblood should be ridden before he is 3 or 3½ years old. We start by introducing young horses to their new surroundings, including the school and the outdoor arena, and familiarize them with lungeing, the bridle and the saddle from about March/April for five or six weeks. Sometimes we ride them briefly. Then, after spending the summer in the field, regular training begins under saddle in the autumn.

We reiterate our view that one must wait until the horse is sufficiently mature, confident and balanced enough before commencing training. We have learned through experience that this is the right line to take in order for training to progress quickly and without problems. Our young horses compete for the first time as 4-year-olds.

An ideal training programme

The best possible conditions to work in, basically follows this pattern:

- 4 years old – Novice level
- 5 years old – Elementary level
- 6 years old – Medium/ Advanced Medium level
- 7 years old – Advanced level.

Training successful horses

Winzerin, Dr Klimke's Olympic eventer in Rome 1960, was bought in 1956 as a 4-year-old. He was ridden straight away. Arcadius also came to the yard as a 4-year-old. He began regular training at the end of his fourth year and in 1962 won the dressage championship for 7-year-olds in Rotterdam. Fabiola was bought as a 2½-year-old and ridden a year later and in 1964 won the German Dressage Derby in Hamburg. Ahlerich, one of the most successful dressage horses of all time, came from the Westphalian auction in Munster. He was bought as a 4-year-old who had hardly been ridden and had competed in just one competition. At 6 he won ten competitions at Medium and Advanced levels, and at 7 won nine Grand Prix competitions. Ahlerich did not have ideal conformation but was very attentive and performed well; with the right assistance from the saddle these exceptional achievements from a young horse are possible.

Ahlerich – Olympic champion in Los Angeles 1984.

The transition from field to stable

When a young horse comes to our yard for ridden training we need to know at least what education he has received so far. We must be familiar with where the horse grew up, what care he has had and what progress he has made. We seldom know every single detail, but can get a good idea of his character by handling him daily. Care is essential in this respect: even with the best information about a new horse he should always be handled with care. This starts from the moment of arrival: unloading from the lorry must be closely supervised and the horse must have the opportunity to be led in hand in walk and trot before being put in his stable. Since the surroundings are new for the horse, it is important that he is handled quietly and confidently in case he becomes worried.

The first impression the horse has of his new surroundings sets a firm precedent for his behaviour in the future. We make sure that he has a deep straw bed, and plenty of hay and fresh water. The next five days is too soon to take on the role of trainer; this is the time to get to know the horse as a groom/rider. In the first week or so it is best if the horse is handled by just one groom, as a variety of handlers can upset a young horse and he can learn to mistrust people.

Horses often come directly from the field to the training yard to be ridden, so a lot of attention must be paid to their diet. Horses coming directly from the field need about 2–2.25 kg of oats (or a suitable feed mix). They need plenty of hay or haylage (about 5.5–7 kg) and plenty of good, clean straw. Carrots (0.5 kg) are a welcome change. We keep an open mind concerning feeding horses – a subject much written about in magazines and books. Nowadays, there is a wide selection of hard feeds on the market and we take the advice of our vet regarding modern improvements in nutrition with regard to vitamins, minerals, feed licks, etc.

For the horse, the change from living in the field to being stabled is very significant. We should not forget that the horse is built for movement. His natural attributes are speed, stamina and agility, which is why sufficient time turned out in the field is very important for the stabled horse. In his book, *The Psychology and Behaviour of the Horse*,

Two-and-a-half-year-old horses enjoying time in the field.

A lively canter out in the fresh air.

Dr Wilhelm Blendiger says that '. . .these days, horses experience problems from having too little exercise rather than too much.'

Young horses who come into the training yard from the field do not have the same amount of room to move around in as they do when spending day and night at grass. Daily turnout in the field or time spent in the paddock is essential. It is important to make sure that the young horse is educated for an hour and has sufficient exercise. This is best divided into two half-hour sessions, one in the morning and one in the afternoon. This routine can begin in the first week after the horse's arrival, once he has settled in and is under control. In this way the horse's trust and self-confidence develop very quickly. In addition to time spent training in the morning the young horse should have a quarter of an hour free in the school, without being chased around, so he can move freely, and in the afternoon the groom should, if possible, lead him in hand from a bridle and take him for a short walk around the stable yard to familiarize him with his surroundings.

At the same time (if the young horse has not been taught these things as a foal), he should learn to be groomed, have his feet picked out and to have his feet and legs washed. The groom should speak quietly to the horse and teach him to react to short words and phrases such as 'come', 'stand', 'foot', 'good boy', etc.

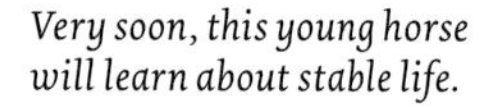

Very soon, this young horse will learn about stable life.

Observing the horse

Generally, we humanize horses too much when dealing with them. Giving bread and sugar at the wrong moment is not to be recommended. By careful observation of the horse as we handle him we learn about his mental state and when to praise him. We must observe his eyes, ears, general expression, tail movements, sweating, neighing, snorting and the way he moves. But what do these mean individually?

Eyes

The horse's temperament and character can be determined from his eyes. A quiet, clear and kind eye indicates a friendly character. Horses with small eyes and a mistrustful look often have difficult temperaments. It is said that a horse with a lot of white in the eye has a lot of energy and can sometimes be difficult.

When the horse's eyes appear uneasy this could indicate that he is nervous, which is understandable when he has been moved to a new yard and has not yet found a person he can trust in this new situation. If the horse has an uneasy look and is agitated even when handled well, this could be an indication of pain, in which case the vet should be called.

Eyes, ears and tail – all indicate the horse's frame of mind!

Fascinated by what's going on.

Ears

The mood of the horse is shown by his ears. If both ears point forward he is in an attentive mood. If the ears are turned to the rear and are apart then he is listening to sounds behind him. If the ears are both laid back slightly then he is worried. Care must be taken if he reacts like this. If the ears are really pressed flat back then he is being defensive and could suddenly bite or kick. He must be spoken to and reprimanded with a short, sharp smack.

Expression

The horse's expression cannot be understood fully just by glancing at him. You need to take time to observe the individual facial features; the movements of the nostrils, lips and ears and the look in his eyes to fully comprehend it, and this one learns from experience. When you have known a horse for a long time and see him every day, you get to know the individual characteristics of his face.

Calm and relaxed.

Tail

Looseness in the way of going, contentment and a quiet rhythm are all indicated by a gently swinging tail. If it is held up stiffly or clamped down it can be a sign of tension in the back, which often happens if the horse becomes excited when leaving his stable.

By allowing the horse to run free in the school for a short while he can get this out of his system and may well enjoy leaping around. When he settles down again his tail will be held normally.

Horses who swish their tails excessively when ridden are often tense. It is important not to ride at too early a stage in spurs, to ride sensitively and also to make sure that the horse works through the back from the beginning.

Voice

Horses use their voices very differently. There are horses one hardly ever hears and those who greet every other horse they see with a loud neigh. The Olympic horse, Dux, used to bring attention to himself all the time by neighing in a loud but friendly manner in unfamiliar situations. This behaviour is most typical of stallions in new surroundings. Young horses frequently neigh at the others back in the stable yard. It is not difficult to teach a horse to greet his rider with a short whinny by bringing a small titbit each time and our food trolley is always greeted by loud neighing.

If a horse groans it is certainly a sign of severe pain, and one should immediately call for assistance.

Squealing is typical of a horse feeling either irritated or playful. This is often heard when two horses are sniffing each other, and it is usually followed by a playful bite or kick. Loud squealing is common from mares in season.

Confident with all that surrounds him.

Snorting

Snorting is a sign of contentment and shows that the horse is relaxed. There is a difference between quick snorting on inhalation when the horse is tense or excited and a longer, relaxed snorting when exhaling. A different form of snorting is small grunts in a different tone in the throat, caused by the vocal cords.

Sweating

Sweat appears naturally when the horse is worked. It is generally an indication of how hard the horse has been working and can thus help in planning the horse's training schedule. However, the time of year and the temperature play a part in the amount a horse sweats. Certain anomalies may also be noted: occasionally, a crooked horse will sweat only on one side, while the other side remains dry, or a horse may sweat only on certain parts of the body, such as the neck. As with people, some horses naturally sweat more than others.

Severe pain such as is indicative of colic will cause sudden and profuse sweating. Young horses can sweat through sheer nervousness; sometimes one can also feel them shaking and the heartbeat is evident just in front of the saddle flaps.

Gaits

The gaits of the horse are a distinguishing feature of his frame of mind and ability. When a young horse first comes out of the stable to run free in the school, for example, it is totally normal for his gaits to be tense. He has to let off steam after being confined to his stable before one can study the quality of his movement.

Assess the young horse as he canters along the short side of the school and see whether he remains balanced or not, which is an indication of the quality of the canter in future ridden work. The mechanics of the trot show the possibilities of developing it further.

A balanced canter.

One could write a long chapter on this alone, drawing conclusions on training methods by observing a horse moving at freedom. Watching the horse completes the picture of what the rider feels and experiences under the saddle. By free-schooling one can see the natural ability of the horse in all three gaits. The gaits can be improved when working with a rider.

Getting the horse used to saddle and bridle

Apart from headcollar and lead-rope, the young horse is unfamiliar with any other equipment. He must get used to it in order that his proper training can proceed. In this phase the horse must absolutely trust his groom, who should therefore feed and groom him daily.

With difficult horses the groom needs to resort to a special way of dealing with things, and that is to have a helper bring the unfamiliar equipment to the stable with food. The helper then holds and feeds the horse while the groom puts on a saddle cloth, roller and brushing boots, in that order.

Care is needed when putting on the saddle cloth and roller to ensure that the latter is fastened gently and not too tightly, so that the horse does not panic and become unsettled.

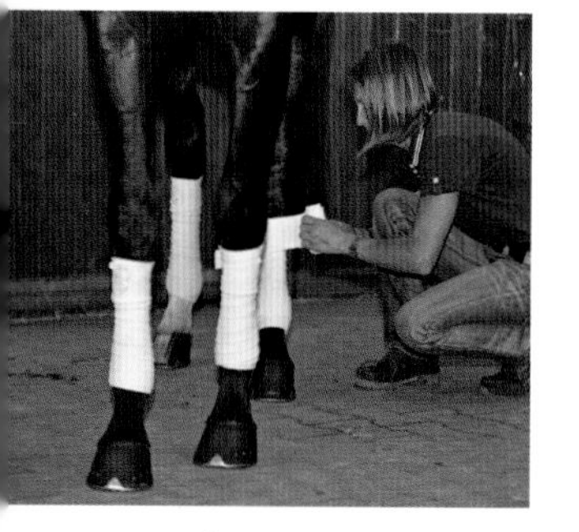

Young horses must get used to having their legs bandaged.

(With young horses one could use either brushing boots or bandages, but the former are better as they can be put on quickly and are easier to clean. Bandages must be washed frequently. During the first winter's work the young horse will not yet have shoes but it is still wise to protect the legs from injuries such as splints and damaged tendons just the same. With horses who brush, specially designed boots offer even better protection.)

Bad habits

It is a bad habit to fasten the noseband too tight. Normally there should be room for two fingers between the noseband and the nasal bone. This keeps the horse's mouth closed but does not restrict him and still allows him to chew the bit. Fastening the noseband too tightly will cause resistance in the horse's mouth, and restrict the flow of air through his nostrils. The sensitivity of the mouth will be compromised and cause the horse to go against the rider's hand.

Fitting the bridle correctly

As with feeding, there are no hard-and-fast rules when it comes to fitting a bridle. In our experience, putting on a bridle for the first time is best done after feeding, when the horse is relaxed. As long as we have ridden horses we have used a simple snaffle bit with a drop or Flash noseband (until they are being prepared for the levels of competition dressage for which a double bridle becomes compulsory) and we will continue to do so, although many other young horses are seen ridden in special bits or bridles.

The drop noseband keeps the horse's mouth closed, preventing him from playing too much with the bit, but allows him the freedom to move his lower jaw and chew the bit. The Flash noseband exerts slight pressure on the nasal bone. This noseband must be fastened sufficiently high (as near as possible to the cheek bone) that, when the rein aids are given, the horse is not pinched between the bit and noseband. Only with a correctly fitted bridle can a horse accept the bit without the risk of developing any mouth problems.

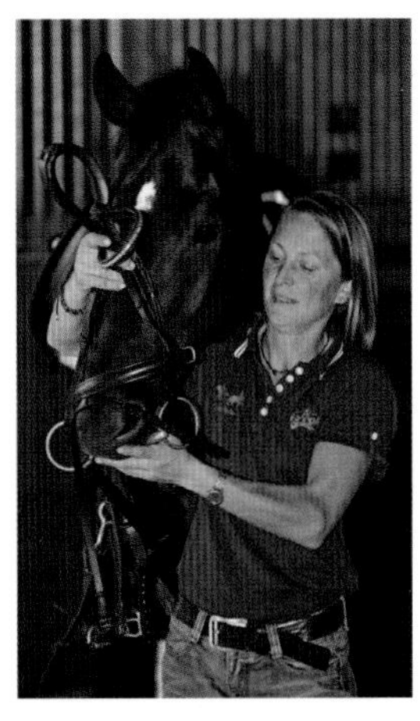

Taking care when putting the bridle on.

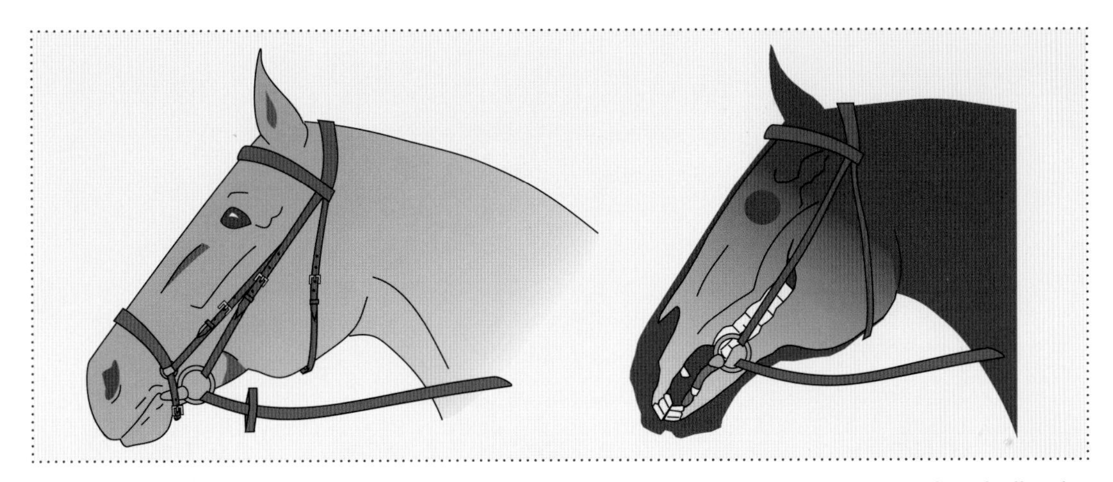

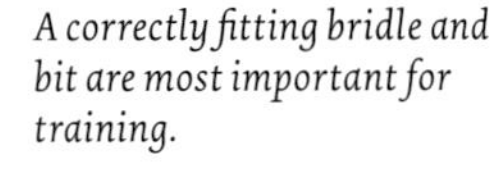

A correctly fitting bridle and bit are most important for training.

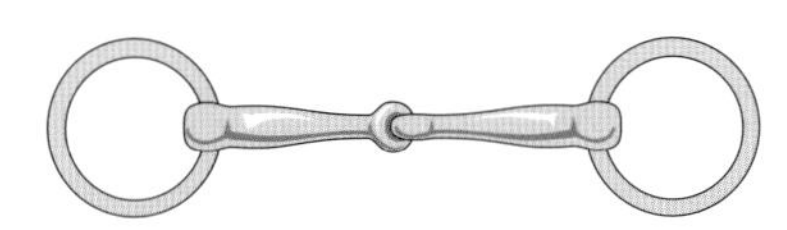

A single-jointed snaffle.

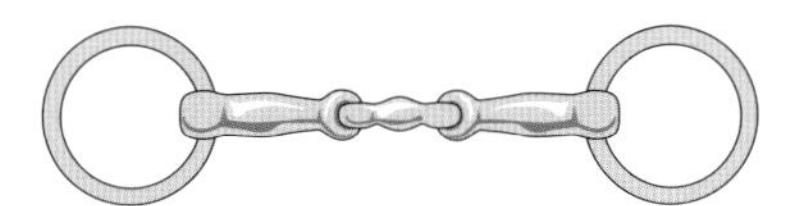

A double-jointed snaffle (training bit with a lozenge in the middle).

The bit must be in the correct position in the horse's mouth. A single- or double-jointed bit (sometimes called a training bit – the double joint has a lozenge in the middle) is the best choice in our opinion. It is important that the tongue has room to move in the mouth and is not restricted by an over-tight noseband. Restriction will simply cause the horse to fight the bit more and a common response to this is to tighten the noseband further as a 'quick fix'. We have corrected various tongue problems by going to the other extreme and using a cavesson noseband fitted as loosely as possible. A correctly fitted bit and soft hands are the best way to correct a tongue problem.

It is also important that a horse with a small mouth is not fitted with a bit that is too fat and that the bridle fits correctly to avoid creating tongue problems.

Saddle

It can be beneficial to put the saddle on initially in the stable, without stirrups or girth. Later the girth can be attached and tightened *gradually*, a little at a time. This prevents any feelings of discomfort or undue restriction on the horse's part, which could lead to a general dislike of being saddled, and reactions such as 'blowing out', cow-kicking, or biting.

The saddle must fit the horse perfectly.

Some trainers accustom the horse to the saddle once he can be led in hand and is already used to a lungeing roller. The different approach is a matter of intuition regarding each individual horse. We always put the saddle on early in the horse's training and lead the horse in hand. Then, when the horse comes to be ridden he is already familiar with it. We use a general purpose saddle on the horse the first time he is ridden and later use special saddles for each discipline such as dressage and jumping.

The saddle must be well made and fit the horse's back properly, so that the rider's weight is correctly distributed and does not cause pressure points. It is a good idea to have the saddle assessed and fitted by a professional before purchase, without a saddle cloth underneath. A tack room full of ill-fitting saddles is a waste of space. The rider must be able to sit correctly in the saddle and ride effectively with flexible hips and a supple back.

Leading in hand

It is customary at stud farms in Germany for young stallions at the end of their second year or beginning of their third to be shown in hand. The mares are 3 years old when assessed for entry in the stud book of the relevant breed society. Ideally, the aim is to appear in hand at the yearly Elite Show. To get there, the horses must have been carefully trained in order that they create a good impression and thus increase their value. Apart from major shows, there are many occasions where the young horse will be required to demonstrate his movement and conformation. In addition to showing in hand (to demonstrate the movement), there is also standing in hand (standing the horse ready for inspection); the standard procedures for which are described below. Traditionally this showing is done using a snaffle bridle, as is the case for other displays later in the horse's career, such as riding horse tests or trotting up to establish soundness in eventing competitions.

Showing in hand can be seen as a simple extension of the training for a horse who is yet to be ridden, and is thus beneficial for a 2-year-old horse as a preparatory exercise for later work under saddle.

Standing for inspection

To stand for inspection the handler should halt the horse (always on level ground) with his shoulders about level with the judge, take a step

This horse could stand with his front legs a bit more 'open'

Walking in hand is fun, and helps the horse develop in maturity.

forward and stand in front of the horse, feet slightly apart. The right rein should be held in the left hand, and the right hand should hold the left rein at about a hand's breadth behind the bit rings. The thumbs have to lie on the reins and the ends of the reins should be coiled and held in the right hand. Finally, the handler must encourage the horse to stand square on all four legs. If he does not do so initially, his stance can be corrected with either a gentle pull to move forwards or soft pressure on the mouth to move slightly backwards. From this stance, the horse should be allowed to take half a step forwards so that he stands straight with all four legs somewhat open so that the judge can see them all clearly. The horse's head and neck should be held slightly forwards (not so much that he hollows his back) so that the quality of the forehand makes an impression.

After showing the horse the handler returns to the left side of the horse and takes the reins in the right hand. The reins should pass between the forefinger and middle finger and be held a good hand's breadth away from the bit rings. The right (outside) rein should be shorter than the left so that the horse's head cannot turn inwards, thus assisting the horse to move straight when he trots. The ends of

Leading in hand successfully...

the reins run from top to bottom through the whole of the right hand and are held in place with the thumb.

Holding the reins correctly when leading in hand.

Ways of leading in hand

To lead the horse in hand at a show there are two possibilities. In Germany, if the horse is judged in an enclosed show ring it is usually triangular. Generally, one is expected to lead up and down the arena in straight lines and at each end the horse should be turned to the right, away from the handler. The horse is shown first in walk and then in trot.

The handler accompanies the horse on the left side, staying about level with the horse's head. The right hand (rein hand) is held at the height of the horse's shoulder; the left arm is left hanging down. In trot the handler must run in time with the horse's steps. If the horse goes too fast he can be steadied by lifting the left hand quietly. A horse will often canter if he is led in trot without any contact on the rein. It is better to keep a light contact so as not to interfere with the rhythm of the trot.

There is a set way to lead in hand. The young horse must be introduced to each single aspect in order to do it properly. We recommend

...depends on how much control you have in your hand.

carrying a long schooling whip. Begin by standing close to the horse's left shoulder and having the rein reasonably long so that the horse will respond to a light contact. The horse is then walked on a long rein in the same way as he learned when he was a foal, so he does not become stressed. It is important to stay by the horse's head and neck and not to get in front of him, and to walk confidently and precisely so that the horse knows exactly what to do and gets no other ideas in his head. Once he is doing this, stand still and quietly say 'halt'. The young horse may take a step further on before stopping, but he must pay attention. If so give a small tug on the rein and immediately slacken it again to avoid any possible resistance from the horse. At this point, pat him briefly on the neck and wait a moment, looking at him. Then look forwards again say, 'come' and walk on. The horse should follow but, if he hesitates, touch him lightly on his hindquarters with the whip.

We repeat this exercise of walking on and halting until the horse understands it well; this usually takes just a few days. We always allow the horse to run free in the school and work off any excess energy by romping around beforehand, then the exercise works without any great problem when he is quiet and relaxed. The day will come, though, when the horse is tense and spooky – and this usually happens when introducing trot. This is a test for the handler's reactions; one must always be quicker than the horse. Sometimes the only way to maintain control is to take a firmer contact on the rein, since it must be very clear to the horse that he must stop and go no further. This firmer hold should not, ideally, involve actually pulling backwards and under no circumstances should the rider hold for too long on the rein as this creates the risk of the horse pulling back. At a later stage, when the horse is more obedient, he can be led and steadied in the approved manner, with the left hand raised quietly in front of his head to steady him before he gets too strong.

When leading lazy horses in hand it helps to have a second person to encourage the horse with the whip, but is wrong to crack it.

Obedience in hand is important preparation for basic training of the riding horse. Young horses who trust people around the stable yard are confident when being introduced to new experiences and always willing to learn something new.

CHAPTER 2

Lungeing and free-schooling

The first stage of lungeing

So far it has been important to observe the horse on a daily basis, but the time comes when the trainer has to be more involved with the horse and commence daily training. The groom is needed as a helper when lungeing and when the horse is ridden for the first time, and when this happens differs from horse to horse. We have known young horses who have been so easy to manage, balanced and trustworthy that they only need to be lunged three or four times before being ridden carefully. On the other hand, an experienced trainer will recognize an unsettled horse and make sure he is lunged several times before a rider sits in the saddle.

Our knowledge of lungeing, which goes back to the work at the Westphalian Riding and Driving School, has been greatly influenced by our own personal experience. While, in this book, we have only covered this theme in relation to basic training and given an outline of the work involved, it is certain that a whole book could be written on the subject. Lungeing supplements and enhances the work of the rider. In our experience work on the lunge has additional functions besides loosening the horse before riding – for example correcting back and neck problems. It is especially useful on non-riding days to give the horse 15–20 minutes work on the lunge to provide some physical exercise and help him to relax mentally.

Details often underestimated

Correct lungeing is as important as correct riding and requires a lot of experience and intuition. A lot of harm can be caused by doing it incorrectly. When first lungeing a young horse the experienced trainer will not follow a rigid training system but will assess the individual needs of each horse.

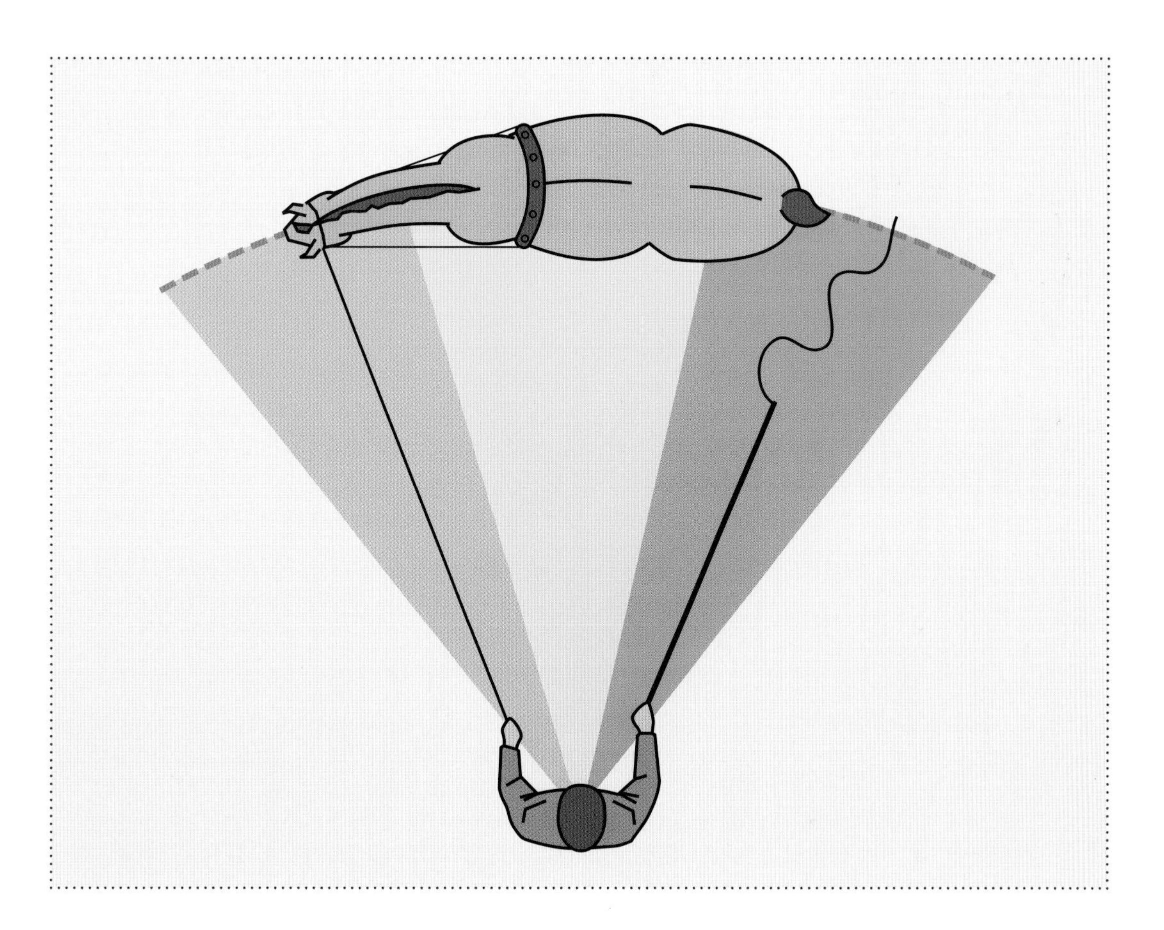

It is useful to lunge on certain days instead of riding so that one can observe the way the muscles move and watch the reactions of the horse to one's aids. Lungeing can complement ridden work by encouraging the horse to track up and work from behind to the bit. This lunge work (without the addition of a rider) should last about 30–40 minutes.

At an earlier stage, work on the lunge prepares the horse for backing and riding. The horse learns through the voice, whip and rein the aids for going forwards and the controlling aids. Co-ordination of the aids when lungeing plays a major role in the same way as when riding (weight, leg and rein aids). The horse learns to take a contact with the bit without leaning on it and to work in balance in all three gaits – walk, trot and, at a later stage, canter on a circle.

Lungeing as part of the basic training

- Lungeing
- Lungeing before ridden work
- Lungeing instead of ridden work (also over cavalletti).

Equipped for training on the lunge.

Lunge equipment

To lunge, apart from the bridle and either boots or bandages we need the following specialized equipment:

- Lunge roller and lunge cavesson
- Running side reins (or plain side reins)
- Lunge rein and lunge whip.

Roller

This should be 15–20 cm wide and padded where it fits across the back in the saddle area. The roller can also be fitted over the saddle. This makes things easier if one intends to ride after lungeing, as the roller just needs to be removed rather than having to switch the roller for the saddle. The roller must have sufficient rings on each side, set both high and low, for the running side reins to be attached to. This is very important in order to accommodate different neck positions depending on the conformation of each individual young horse.

Cavesson

A well-padded noseband is essential to prevent the cavesson rubbing. There should be three rings on the noseband and the lunge line should be fastened to the middle one. With horses who pull to the outside the inner ring can be used to prevent the cavesson from slipping to one side.

The full cavesson is complicated to fit properly and it can be a long procedure for a young horse. First, the horse is tacked up using a snaffle bridle. The cavesson is fastened over the bridle with the headpiece and browband over the corresponding parts of the bridle. The throatlash of the cavesson must be fastened securely so that its cheekpieces do not slide around and touch the eyes – which the person lungeing will not be able to see on the outside of the horse's face.

It is much easier to use a simpler version of the cavesson which consists of a noseband with three rings on it and a throatlash. We prefer this with young horses as they do not feel encumbered with too many straps around the head.

With a correctly fitted cavesson the rein aids with the lunge line act on the nasal bone without risking injury to the mouth. The young horse should be comfortable with the bit and not get pulled in the mouth – which can sometimes happen unintentionally when the horse is spooky and jumping around. When lungeing from a cavesson the trainer can give clear and effective rein aids without worrying about injuring the mouth.

Lunge line

Rather than being attached to the cavesson, the lunge line can alternatively be attached to the inside bit ring of the bridle. If this method is used, care must be taken that the bit is not pulled through the horse's mouth when the side reins are very long. It is wrong to thread the rein through the inside bit ring, pass it under the chin and fasten it to the outer bit ring because this can cause the bit to pinch the corners of the mouth. As mentioned above, our preference is to use either a cavesson or a drop noseband and to clip the lunge line to the bit and the noseband ring.

Running side reins

Side reins are a substitute for the rider's hands. Running side reins are plain leather reins which pass from the girth, through the bit rings, and fasten to the saddle on either side. In our opinion running side reins are better than fixed side reins as they encourage the horse to

A roller with running side reins. The different rings on the roller allow them to be attached in a variety of ways. The horse's head must be in front of the vertical.

1

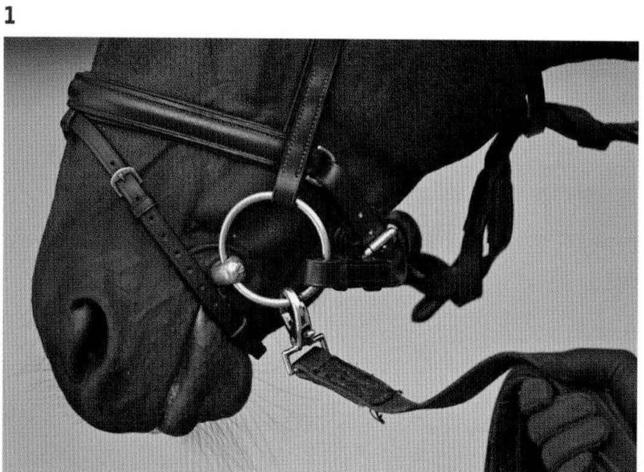

2

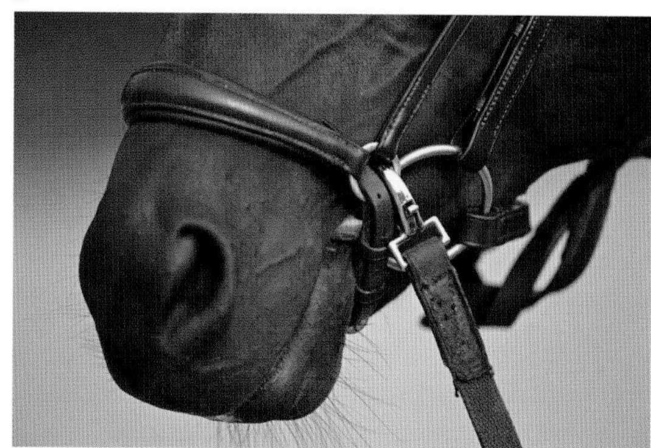

1 *Fastening the lunge rein to the inside bit ring.*

2 *Fastening the lunge rein to the bit ring and the ring on the drop noseband.*

stretch forwards and downwards more and help the horse to seek a gentle contact with the bit. Many trainers are of the opinion that rubber inserts in fixed side reins give a little to prevent the horse from setting against the bit, but we have not had this experience. One can compare the give in the side reins with a softening of the rider's wrists, but some horses tend to lean on side reins with rubber or elastic inserts and do not learn to accept a light contact with the bit. We fasten the running side reins long enough so that the horse can move freely forward in walk and, with young horses, both reins are often set at the same length. The advantage of this is that the outside rein gives the horse a contact and the inside rein becomes softer when the horse is encouraged to give by gentle actions of the lunge line attached to the inside bit ring. Later on, the inside rein can be shortened by two or three holes when working on a circle.

As training progresses and more bending and contact are required then the side reins should be shortened. The length is determined by the size of the horse and how his neck is set on. The outside rein is fastened so that his head carriage remains steady, controlling the amount of flexion to the inside and preventing the horse from escaping through his outside shoulder.

There is another way of attaching side reins. At the Westphalian Riding and Driving School the schoolmaster horses were ridden by the younger riders in side reins that were crossed under the neck, that is the right side rein was fastened to the left bit ring, and the left side rein to the right bit ring. The side reins were as long as possible to allow the horse to flex at the poll (rather than being over-shortened, which could

Long or short

Normally young horses should be lunged with long side reins at first, which should be progressively shortened. With older horses, they are fastened at a shorter length first according to the horse's neck carriage and lengthened to encourage him to stretch forwards and down as he relaxes and loosens up. The nose should never come behind the vertical, and the reins should not be shortened or lengthened more than two to four holes in total.

This is how it should look: with the nose just in front of the vertical.

provoke flexing behind the poll). Without worrying about their hands the young riders could concentrate on the feel of the horses' backs and learn to sit correctly. The side reins did not need to be altered when changing direction in the school.

Lunge line and whip

The lunge line is about 7 or 8 m long and has a hand loop at the end. There are lunge lines that are up to 10 m in length which have the advantage of allowing the horse to work on a very large circle. The lunge whip should be light and long enough so that the trainer can reach the horse with the end of the lash. The whip should not be laid on the ground but carried under the arm when not in use.

Using the aids

The co-ordination of the aids (voice, whip and lunge line) is vital to the quality and efficiency of work on the lunge. *One can tell much about the training routine, sensitivity and experience of any trainer by the horse's response to the aids.*

Horses learn to respond to your voice when you always use the same tone of voice. It can help to put a list of commands in the tack room for everyone to follow. These words should also be familiar to

The aids

Voice aids

- From halt to walk 'walk on'.
- From walk to trot 'ter-rot'.
- From trot to canter 'and canter'.
  (Raising the tone of your voice is important in the upward transitions.)
- From canter to trot 'and ter-rot.'
- From trot to walk 'and walk'.
- From walk to halt 'ha-alt'(without the horse falling in).
  (Lower the tone of your voice in the downward transitions.)

Whip aids

- Use in the direction of the hind hoof as a subtle driving aid.
- Use in the direction of the croup for normal forward-driving aid.
- Move it from the croup towards the forehand to drive forwards strongly.
- Flick the horse just above the hock to encourage him to step under and forwards.

Aids with the lunge line

- Hold the line lightly when the horse takes a gentle contact.
- Use a soft contact/side reins to give enough control over the gaits and the tempo.
- Taking a firm contact regulates the tempo and asks the horse to step backwards.
- Giving encourages acceptance of the contact.

riders who are used to riding as a group in the school. Old horses are reassured by them and young horses learn them very quickly.

The voice aid is by far the most important of the three aids (voice, whip and lunge line). At the Westphalian Riding and Driving School there was a mare called Sirka who was so responsive to the voice that she would walk, trot and canter all on her own. If one said 'stand' from outside the school, Sirka would halt.

Recipe for success

Is it time to begin lungeing the horse?

By being patient and waiting for the right time future progress will be quicker.

Lungeing before the initial mounting and riding

For the first lunge session to progress successfully the horse must be able to concentrate. Therefore, this is best done in the indoor school, making sure there are no obstacles left in the arena. If there

Working 'long and low' in a relaxed trot.

is only an outdoor school to use, make sure that two or three sides of the circle are enclosed by fences or hedges. It can be helpful to enclose the lungeing area fully with a properly constructed barrier of jump stands and poles.

Do not use the lunge whip to start with. On the first day let the horse run free in the school to allow him to blow off steam after being in his stable and afterwards ask your helper to assist with putting on the lunge equipment. Some trainers do not yet connect the running side reins, and others fasten them loosely, but they should not be so long that there is a risk of them causing an accident. The weight of the reins should be sufficient at first to encourage the horse to reach for a contact.

The helper walks on the outside of the horse on the left rein, leading him by the cheekpiece, while the trainer walks along on the inside of the horse, holding the lunge line in the left hand without influencing the horse at this stage. The right hand remains free to pat the horse from time to time. After a couple of circuits the trainer gradually lengthens the lunge line and moves to the middle of the circle. The trainer then stands in one place, turning to follow the movement of the horse as he moves around on a circle, and carefully takes up a contact with the lunge rein. Now is the time for the helper to let go and allow the horse to go alone on the circle. This should be repeated on the right rein: walk, halt, and pat. The horse should halt on the circle and be praised when he does so. It can help to reward him with a handful of oats or pieces of carrot. The first lunge session should last no longer than 30 minutes.

Young trainers tend to be impatient the first time and work the horse for too long as they want to progress quickly. A good trainer will take care that the pupil does no more than he can cope with, and be pleased with any progress shown. On the next day it is very important that the horse is praised a lot and worked quietly again.

We make progress

On the next day the lunge whip can be introduced. The exercise begins as the previous day. The trainer carries the whip so that it points towards the horse's inside hind foot, making a triangle with the lunge line and the whip. The helper leads the horse by the cheekpiece to reassure him in case he becomes frightened. Then the horse is asked to trot quietly forwards with the voice aid as the helper lets go of the bridle and moves to the inside of the horse, near to the saddle area. As soon as the trainer has control of the horse with the whip the helper can drop back, allowing the trainer to take over fully.

The trainer uses the whip towards the horse's croup when necessary. It is important at a later stage to touch the horse just above

When adjusting the side reins, the lunge whip should be placed under your arm.

the hock and say, 'come' to encourage him to go forwards. If the horse is fresh allow him to do a few circuits in trot until he relaxes and settles. The horse will walk again when he is ready, and the trainer must be prepared to wait a while for this to happen.

The second training session on the lunge is successful when the horse has learned to go alone around the circle in trot from a touch of the whip and the voice aid. The session should last no longer that 30 minutes and finish in walk. It is too early to ask for canter at this stage.

It is important to lunge the horse on both reins but we begin on the left rein as this is easier for the horse. Most horses bend more easily to the left because of their natural crookedness (with those horses crooked to the right the left hind foot does not step in the direction of the left forefoot but in between the forelegs to step more under the centre of gravity). With the majority of horses, starting on the right rein can cause problems such as turning in or spinning around in the opposite direction, depending on the temperament of the horse.

The first time we change the rein the same helper is required to assist; each horse should be handled and treated as an individual. As a rule of thumb the horse should be able to work on the lunge in walk and trot on both reins at the earliest after three to four days, and the latest seven to eight days.

Now is the time to begin the proper work on the lunge so that the horse becomes safe and obedient enough for backing and riding to commence. The trainer must have the feeling and impression that the horse is immediately responsive to the aids. The aids of the lunge whip are a substitute for the rider's legs and schooling whip. The rein aids are simulated by the lunge line, cavesson and side reins (although, before starting canter work, the running side reins should initially be removed so as not to disturb the rhythm or shorten the stride).

To develop the canter we ask the horse to go into a quiet trot and then, with the whip and the voice command, 'and canter', allow the horse to step into the canter by giving slightly with the lunge line. Three or four circuits in this gait are enough. After cantering, the horse should be allowed to come to a quiet trot, and then walk.

Lungeing is deemed successful when the young horse goes with his neck reaching forwards and down to the bit with appropriately

Maintaining inside flexion with a steady contact on the lunge rein.

Less is more

Several short spells of canter improve canter strides on a circle better than longer sessions.

A happy expression; the girth should be loosened after work.

adjusted side reins, and can quietly walk, trot and canter on a large circle. This should be attainable in about two to three weeks, depending on the individual horse's progress.

To enable the trainer to ride the horse as soon as possible we must reiterate that the horse should be lunged at least three or four times before backing, but with an unsettled horse seven or eight times will be necessary.

Free-schooling in the indoor arena

My father told me that at the Westphalian Riding and Driving School the young horses were free-schooled in the small indoor school at about the time lunge work commenced and before they were ridden. This was done without side reins at first, but with them at a later stage. The 20m x 40m school enabled the trainer to stay in close contact with the young horse with voice and the whip. If such a procedure is to be followed, any mirrors on the walls must be securely fixed to avoid injury and four plastic blocks, one in each corner, will help to keep the horse on the track.

It is an advantage to watch the young horse running free. It is much easier for him to loosen up without the restriction of the lunge rein. However, moving free in the school can feel so good to the horse that he may become very excited and gallop around, in which case the

Free-schooling is very enjoyable – plastic blocks prevent the horse from cutting the corners.

alternative would be to work him on the lunge. Some horses may run into a corner and stop. Such horses should be encouraged to turn right or left by approaching them to one side and using the voice and whip aids from a safe distance.

Loosening up exercise

We stand four plastic blocks, one in each corner, about 2 m in from the track. The horse is led into the school wearing brushing boots, bridle and a saddle or roller. Free-schooling in a saddle accustoms the horse to moving with the saddle in place and is an alternative to lungeing with tack on as a preparation for riding. However, the saddle must be a comfortable fit for the horse and it is inadvisable to place a cold saddle suddenly on the back of a warm horse; this can cause bucking and 'fireworks' and is unwise if you intend to ride him straight afterwards. The girth needs to be sufficiently tight to prevent the saddle from slipping but, as always, it should be tightened gradually before the free-schooling begins. The running side reins are laid in the middle of the school and the stirrups run up and secured. The bridle reins are twisted and the throatlash passed between them to keep them secure and out of the way.

As the horse can tend to be rather exuberant after being in the stable it is a good idea to watch him from the middle of the school once the free-schooling begins. The young horse will stop after 5–10 minutes and should be caught quietly, spoken to and rewarded with pieces of carrot, etc. This encourages a bond between trainer and horse, and makes it easier for next time.

Free-schooling with running or fixed side reins

The horse is now ready for more serious work. The side reins are put on as loosely as possible and the same length on both sides, so that he can find a light contact. The running side reins hold the bit quietly in place so that the young horse learns to trust the bit and reach for the contact without leaning on it. This helps the horse to reach forwards and down with his neck and loosen up through his back. Reins that are too short can cause resistance through the neck. Having the running side reins the same length helps to keep the horse straight as opposed to lungeing on a circle, where the inside rein is shortened.

The beginning of the work phase with the horse in an outline.

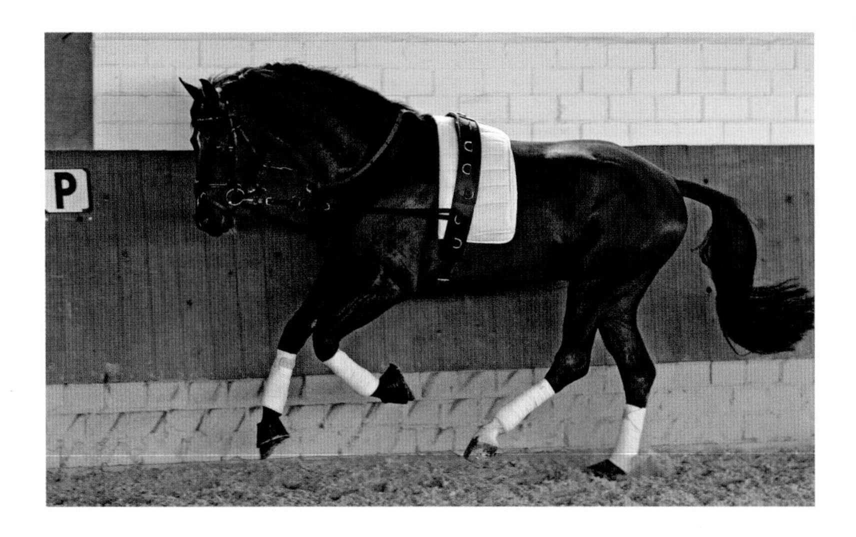

With the running side reins fastened the young horse should be allowed to run free in the school, but he must stay in trot or canter. After a short time we must watch out for the horse falling in from the wall, when he will need the help of the trainer and/or assistant and the four blocks (one in each corner) to keep him on the track. Some horses are happy to go along by the wall after about 5 minutes whereas others need more time and a second helper in the arena. When running free in the school, some young horses can fall out and lean towards the wall for support. It may be useful to move nearer the horse in this instance to give him confidence. The lunge whip can be used towards the croup to encourage him to keep moving forwards. We are happy when a horse can remain balanced in trot in an even tempo and step forwards and under and lengthen his stride. The quieter the trainer and assistant(s), the calmer the horse will be. As the horse moves freely around the school it is a good opportunity to study his character, intelligence and way of moving; whether he is willing and quick to pick things up, or whether he is obstinate. At the same time this is also a good test of one's own patience and ability to remain calm throughout the stages of basic training – and looking ahead to future competitions.

The training session is concluded after about 20 minutes. The side reins are removed and the horse walked for a while until he is breathing normally again. He is rewarded with oats or carrots and then taken back to his stable.

Rewarding the horse with food lets him know he has done well.

CHAPTER 3

Training under saddle

Riding for the first time

A lot of skill and experience are required when mounting a young horse for the first time. The quietest horse can spook when a large shadow appears above him and he feels an unfamiliar weight on his back. It is recommended that a rider who is able to sit lightly and securely sits on the horse for the first time.

The young horse must quietly learn to carry the rider's weight by using all his muscles, particularly his back, neck and abdominal muscles to support his spine. With an untrained horse these are obviously not strong enough. Stiffness in the back and neck, running forwards, leaning on the reins, stumbling and other problems in self-carriage and the gaits are common occurrences at first. For these reasons, it is important not to be too ambitious to begin with, and to be satisfied with familiarizing the horse with mounting, dismounting and the rider's weight in the saddle.

Getting the horse used to mounting and dismounting

There are trainers who get the horse used to mounting and dismounting in the stable. We think this is an extremely cautious method and have done it only in exceptional circumstances. To do it in this way, the horse must first be lunged from the bridle and then led back into his box with the saddle still on, and he should be facing the manger. The helper should stand next to the left side of the horse and hold the left rein with the left hand. The reins should be over the horse's neck. The rider approaches and reaches up with the left hand as though grooming the horse. As soon as the horse accepts this, the helper puts their right hand under the rider's lower left leg and carefully gives the rider a leg up. If the horse is quiet, the rider swings the right leg over the horse's back and sits gently in the saddle, leaning forwards slightly so as not to alarm the horse. A moment later the rider dismounts in exactly the same way. From a safety angle the rider must

The full concentration of everyone involved is essential when mounting a horse for the first time!

wear a riding hat with a chinstrap. This exercise can be repeated a few times, rewarding the horse on each occasion, after which it can be repeated in the indoor school.

Normally, mounting and dismounting are practised in the indoor school after the horse has first been prepared with a thorough lungeing session, or by free-schooling. On the day that he is to be ridden the young horse should be lunged on both reins so that he is a little tired when the rider is lifted into the saddle. For safety, the horse can wear a neck strap for the rider to hold onto in case he jumps around a bit. The lungeing gear is left on the horse after the helper has lunged him. A second helper then gives the rider a leg up and the rider lies over the saddle, remaining in this position while the helper pats the horse. After a short time the rider slides back down to the ground. This exercise should be repeated a few times so that the horse becomes familiar with the rider's weight on his back. Next, the rider lifts their right leg over the horse's back and sits in the saddle. The upper body must lean slightly forwards, with the hands holding the neck strap.

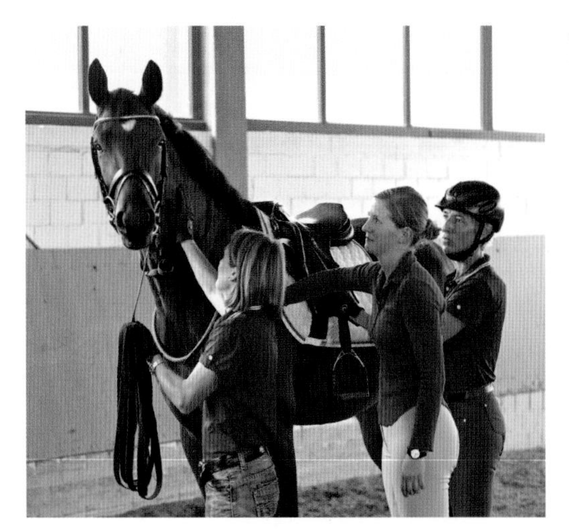

Quietly praising the horse reassures him.

'What is going on now?'

In my experience, there is little difficulty in leading the horse forwards as soon as the rider is in the saddle. The groom leads the horse on the now familiar large circle. If the horse becomes tense he should be halted and patted to reassure him before continuing. Again, this should be repeated several times. For most horses, getting used to the rider's weight in walk on the first day is quite sufficient.

After repeating the same training on the second day, the horse should be ready to trot on the lunge. He should first be led around the school for a short time by the groom while the rider remains passive in the saddle in a light seat. The rider must assess whether the horse should be either walked or trotted for a short time, but this varies with each individual horse. Ideally, the horse should be quiet enough to do this after a couple of sessions just practising mounting and dismounting.

Riding the horse for the first time can be made easier by having a lead horse in the arena. After the young horse has been lunged first, the second horse is brought quietly into the arena so that the young horse can follow him. This can be helpful a couple of times to give him confidence.

The rider on the lead horse should keep a horse's length in front of the youngster and ride quietly forward in walk as soon as the rider of the young horse is in the saddle. This works best on the track on the left rein. This removes the risk of the young horse falling out through the outside shoulder, which he could do if ridden on a circle at this stage. (The person who lunged the horse prevents him falling in by remaining on the inside of the horse.) After a few steps of walk, a short trot can be introduced. Future sessions should be attempted without the lead horse after the youngster has been accustomed to mounting, dismounting and short spells in trot.

The first ride.

In walk with a leader close to the horse while another person keeps control with the lunge rein.

Getting used to the rider's weight

The introduction of the rider's weight in the saddle comes after the horse has been properly loosened up and prepared by lungeing for 10–15 minutes, mounting and dismounting, stretching the legs, and leading in hand over poles either on the ground or raised slightly. Even so, over the next few days, consideration must be given as to whether the horse is really ready to take a rider's weight yet. It is certainly better to wait at least a couple of weeks before introducing any new work under saddle. Also, we do not ride the young horses every day, but use non-riding days for gymnastic work – free-schooling, simple lungeing, or cavalletti work on the lunge – to build the muscles required to carry the rider's weight. Tension in the back, neck and abdominal muscles is normal in the beginning; relaxation comes as the muscles become stronger.

Because the young horse's back muscles under the saddle are not developed at this stage, the saddle can tend to slip. Therefore, at each rest period it should be adjusted so that it sits correctly. The saddle area will develop over time. In certain circumstances this can take a month or so depending on the conformation of the horse's withers and shoulders. Breeding has improved this in recent times so, in general, the saddle area of many youngsters is better than used to be the case and a fore-girth (to prevent the saddle slipping forwards) is seldom required.

Muscle building

The back muscles are not strengthened by long spells of work. Muscles can only be built by strengthening them in their natural functions. There is certainly a risk of damage to immature muscles if they are worked too much too soon.

In the first few weeks, after the horse has initially become used to the rider, he can be ridden in rising trot. If ridden in canter, the rider

A later stage: the first trot on the lunge.

should assume a light, or forward, seat. The hands remain in position either side of the horse's neck and maintain a light contact with his mouth. If the horse becomes unsteady or restless the knees should be quickly and firmly closed. The rider then holds the neck strap with one hand and avoids holding tightly onto the reins. Should the young horse become anxious and speed up the experienced rider should calm him by speaking to him quietly until he steadies down.

Going forward in trot around the school.

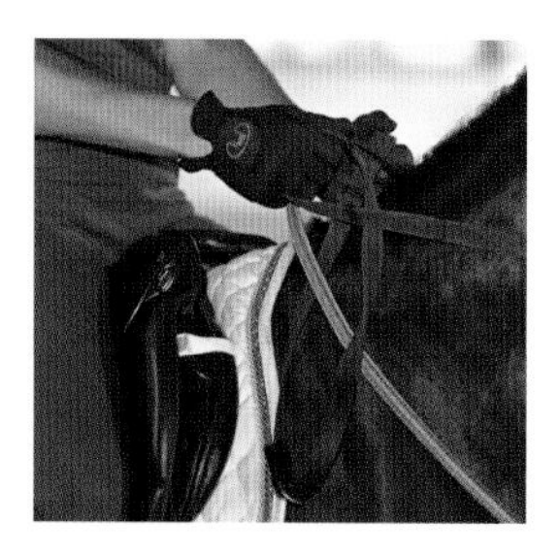

Using a neck strap for security.

Riding in a light seat – off the horse's back – in an uphill canter.

Should anything happen that causes the young horse to buck and unseat the rider, the rider should get back into the saddle immediately so that the horse does not get the opportunity to think that this is a good way to get rid of the weight on his back.

When riding a young horse the rider must be able to move with him without restricting his movement. The rider must have the initiative to familiarize the horse with the aids, controlling the tempo with the voice and, when necessary, a short whip.

The whip should be used on the shoulder, as some horses may resent a whip aid behind the rider's leg at this stage. The spurs should be left in the tack room; they are not necessary at this time.

We are satisfied when the youngster can walk and trot on both reins for about 10–15 minutes after being mounted, using a quiet lead horse if necessary. We remain on straight lines or follow the lead horse on a large circle. The young horse should not be ridden for any longer than 20 minutes at a time during the first week but this should gradually be extended in the second week to about 30 minutes, taking in two or three rest periods in walk before changing the rein. When a horse can carry a rider's weight willingly in walk and trot, the initial training has been successful.

The development of basic training

During the next phase of training the horse learns to accept the rider's aids without suffering physical injury or mental stress. The Scales of Training, which outline the correct phases of education necessary to achieve this, are:

1 Rhythm
2 Suppleness
3 Contact
4 Impulsion
5 Straightness
6 Collection

The horse should work through his back from the first stage of riding, and this is helped by riding half-halts and transitions into and out of trot, for example.

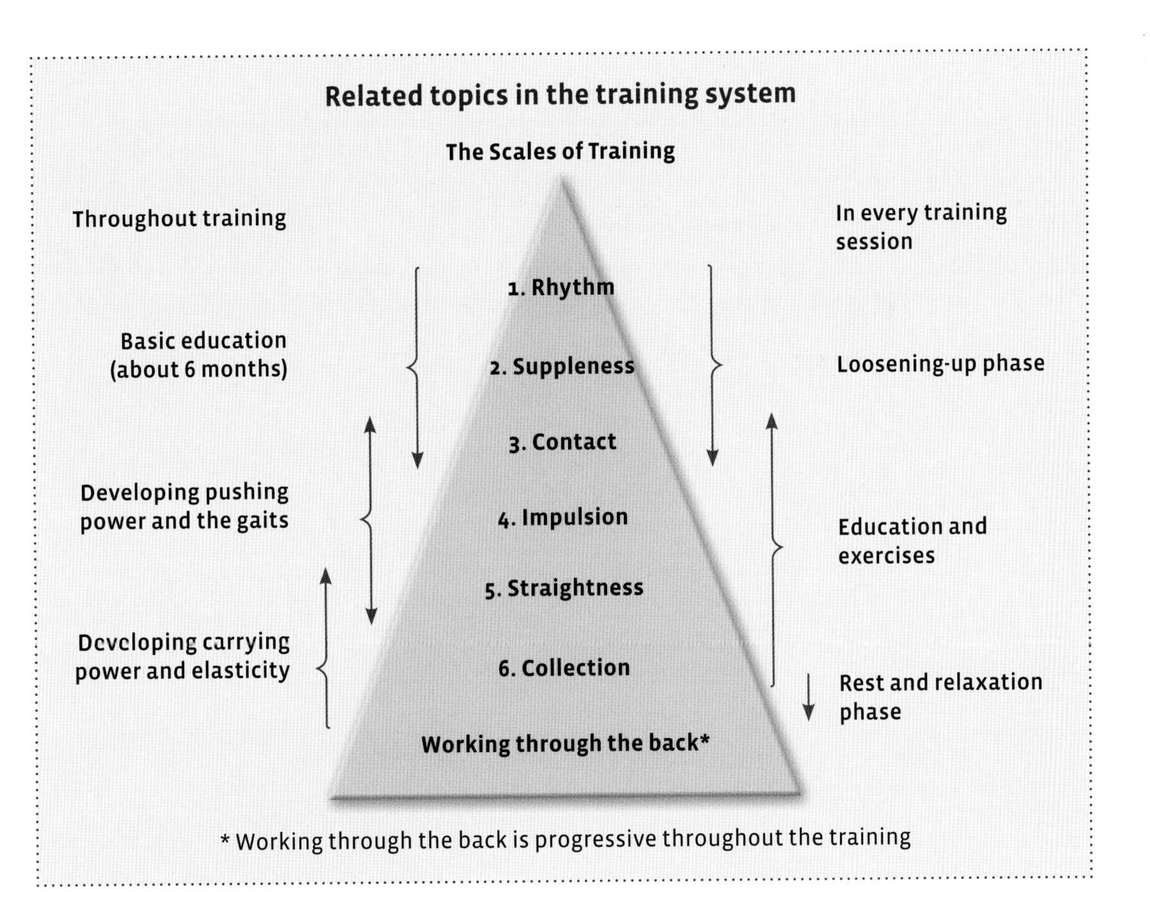

Working through the back is not mentioned in the Scales of Training despite the fact that well-known trainers of the German cavalry practised and taught it. It was said that understanding the horse was the key to acceptance of the rider's aids (submission). The horse should accept the driving aids (legs and seat) without resistance and with active hind legs develop pushing power and, at a later stage, be able to carry weight behind. He should also accept a contact with the reins, flexing through the poll, top line of the neck and back, allowing the hindquarters to tuck under the body, which is achieved through halts and half-halts using the co-ordinated weight, leg and rein aids. In every stage of training the horse must work through his back.

Used correctly, the Scales of Training (or ground rules) help to develop the natural ability of the horse. When progress is delayed by resistance or confrontation the rider must remain self-disciplined. The horse can only reach the required level of training and work correctly through his back with the influence of the rider's aids. Basic training must be established before concentrating on individual ambitions.

Rhythm

What does this mean? The horse has three basic gaits: walk, trot and canter. Each of these gaits has a set sequence of footfalls: the walk is four-beat, the trot two-beat and the canter three-beat. The regularity of the steps while maintaining the natural movement of the horse is described as rhythm. Maintaining rhythm is an important task for riders of young horses. The rider must go quietly with the movement of the horse and help him to find his natural balance before asking him to adjust his balance under the rider's weight. The horse must learn to carry the weight of the rider so that he can move freely in a relaxed manner again. When this is possible the horse is described as moving in natural balance and in a rhythm.

Active or passive?

Active hind legs, a supple back, improved outline and better movement of the horse are achieved by asking with half-halts and not by just waiting for them to happen.

Suppleness

By this we understand the swinging of the back as the centre of movement and the contraction and extension of the required muscles without tension (i.e. in the neck, the back, between the ribs and in the hindquarters).

A lovely trot – forward, unrestricted and in balance.

As well as appearing outwardly supple, there must also be contentment and 'inner calm' or willingness on the inside. The inner qualities of the horse are temperament, character, friendliness, sensitivity, trainability, willingness, and natural ability. Responsiveness to the rider's aids is dependent on age and stage of training. We must then help the young horse to work with the unfamiliar weight of a rider on his back so that he can complete his education. He must develop the ability to work as freely and naturally with the rider in the saddle as without.

Contact

With the subsequent development of carrying power of the hindquarters the horse is more able to work through his back into a steadier contact with the bit. Swinging movement under the rider can only be achieved when a secure, soft contact can be maintained between the rider's hands and the horse's mouth. One can see spectacular movement when horses run free. Improvement of natural impulsion can only be achieved when a soft, elastic, steady, feeling contact exists.

A secure, light contact.

A soft contact between the rider's hand and the horse's mouth.

The horse should step towards the bit and, through his individual length of stride and stage of training, maintain the desired outline. In this outline his strength is best developed, but this is dependent on first achieving the correct contact.

Impulsion and straightness

The correct contact improves rhythm, suppleness, the ability to work through the back and impulsion. The horse works expressively and actively under the rider when he is allowed to step energetically forwards with his hind feet. Propulsive power is developed in trot and canter when it is transferred forwards through the horse's swinging back. This is described in basic training as developing impulsion.

'Ride the horse forwards and straight' is an important training objective of Gustav Steinbrecht in his *The Gymnasium of the Horse*, which has been around for many years. 'Make your horse flexible on both sides, ride him forward and straight' was the phrase of Major a.D. Paul Stecken, the long-serving manager of the Westphalian Riding and Driving School.

Nearly all young horses have a problem going straight, some more so than others. This is a consequence of the natural crookedness of the horse. In the same way that most people are right-handed, so most horses are crooked from the right hind to the left fore, i.e. the right hind foot does not step into the print of the right forefoot, but away to the right. In his book, *Riding Logic*, Wilhelm Müseler discusses the theory that crookedness depends on which way the foal laid in his mother's womb. Through basic training natural crookedness can be improved by building the horse up equally on both sides and improving flexibility through the rib cage on both sides so that both hind legs step on the same line as the corresponding forelegs, that is *the hind legs follow in the tracks of the forelegs*. This applies both to straight lines and to circles and curved figures such as serpentines.

Maintaining equal weight on all four legs in certain exercises is also absolutely essential for maintaining quality of movement and the health of the horse.

Cantering easily on a curved line.

Collection

After about a year it is time to start working towards collection. This entails the horse taking more of the weight on the hindquarters, coiling the loins by closing the pelvis, hip and stifle joints and thus shifting his centre of gravity backwards. In this way the horse can produce more power. Also, the more weight the hind legs can take, the freer the shoulder movement is, and the lighter forehand places less strain on the forelegs.

The benefits of collection do not apply only to dressage but also to jumping (for example when turning, or preparing before an obstacle such as a water jump) and even to hacking. Moreover, certain dressage movements can only be ridden out of collection where the forehand is lightened in preparation, for example extended trot or canter or voltes in canter.

The raising of the forehand by collection also allows improvement in working through the back. However, it is important to understand that the lifting of the forehand is dependent on the lowering of the haunches. False lifting of the forehand happens when the rider lifts the horse with the hands, the horse going against the reins. There is then no stepping under of the hind legs.

The development of relative elevation of the forehand.

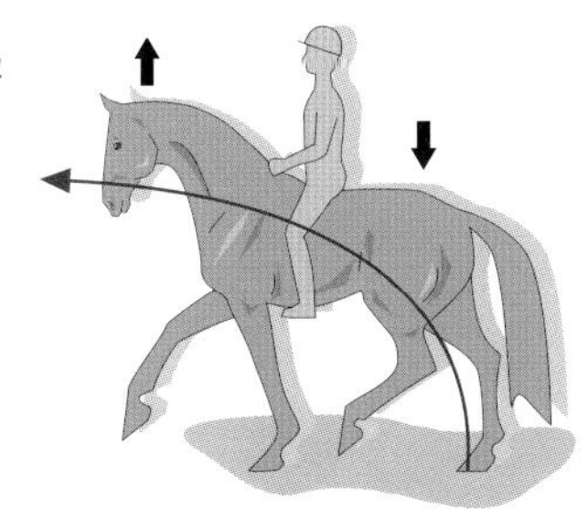

Working through the back

A rider who wants more influence over the horse's movement must work to use the aids to ride the horse forwards and develop the lateral

The pushing power of the haunches develops from a swinging back.

movements. Obedient response to these aids will help develop the working through the back. As the young horse's ability to work through the back develops it is possible to ride transitions and simple exercises in rhythm with him. Alternatively, without this suppleness developing, the energy from the hind legs cannot swing forwards through the whole horse. It is necessary to be aware that strong rein

The test of working into a secure contact is to release the inside rein by taking the hand gently forward.

aids cause tension in the poll, neck or back, preventing the hindquarters from working correctly.

The progressive benefits of the young horse working through the back can be summarized thus:

- A horse with a supple back can step forwards energetically with his hind feet, is able to react to the driving and controlling aids and can go forwards with good impulsion in trot and canter.
- A horse who works through the back is able to react to half-halts and respond to the forward-driving aids on both sides of his body, moving straight towards the rider's hands without the hindquarters swinging away to one side. (Extending the trot and canter strides can be improved by rein-back.)
- Working through the back is essential for exercises such as walk–canter and canter–walk. Also for the exercise trot–halt–rein-back and riding forwards once more, resulting in improvement of the degree of collection and lifting of the forehand.

Working through the back, which is achieved with correct training, makes it easier for the horse to obey the aids, thus making things easier for both horse and rider. The rider must not be inconsistent in

A further stage is to 'stroke the horse's neck' by taking both hands forward.

Ridden work in walk at the beginning of a training session should ideally be done on a loose rein.

the aids. There should be a partnership between horse and rider. The horse should chew the bit quietly and carry his tail in a quiet, relaxed manner. There should be harmony between horse and rider in their daily training!

Planning a ridden session

Basic training sets us on the right track to develop the natural ability of the horse. It is wrong to believe that with a 4-year-old horse one can achieve looseness in one session, rhythm in the next, and then contact, etc. This is simply not the case. The individual elements of training develop side by side and as a trainer one should ensure that they are present whether the horse is destined for dressage, jumping or hacking. Basic training lays the foundation for the future development of the horse while maintaining his trust.

Introducing new exercises depends on the individual ability of each horse. Repeating the same exercise relentlessly is monotonous and should be avoided. A ridden session should be planned so that it has a variety of movements which cover all the elements of training. Weather and facilities permitting, we like to begin by loosening the horse up over cavalletti (see Chapter 6) and going for a short hack after the training session, or else going for a hack before riding some dressage exercises in the school. Sometimes we loosen the horse up by cantering in a light seat on straight lines around the exterior of the school before going into the school itself. This preparatory work must be fun for both horse and rider, in fact it goes without saying that it must be a good experience for the horse so that he is calm and prepared for training. Every session is made up of three parts: loosening up, working, and walking to end with. For the young horse this means loosening up, working and further loosening. Loosening up in walk, trot and canter to get rid of any tension is essential before the rider can drive the horse forwards. With older horses (more than 5 years old) loosening up should last about 15–20 minutes.

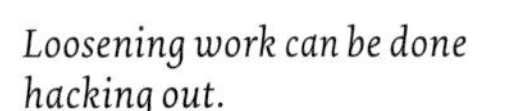

Loosening work can be done hacking out.

The aim of daily training for a young horse (about 4 years old) is to make him completely supple. In the first half-year, a 4-year-old horse is loosened up with different lessons and exercises. In the second half-year more difficult exercises are introduced to improve rhythm, suppleness, contact and especially working through the back. The next stage is to introduce a variety of exercises, some easier than others, using the training already established in the first and second half-year periods. Exercises in the third and fourth half-years of training should introduce collected work that will be ridden more towards the end of that period (at about 5–6 years of age) so that all aspects of training are covered.

Many horses prefer loosening up in canter.

Suppling exercises in the first year

The following simple loosening exercises are suitable for 3- to 4-year-old horses in the first five to six months of training:

1. As a general rule, about 10 minutes in walk on a loose rein. For safety reasons young horses who have only just started ridden work should only be ridden on a contact, but without flexion at the poll. Horses in whom the four-beat walk is not properly established, those who overbend slightly, or have poll problems, should be worked on a long rein in order to control flexion in the poll area.
2. Rising trot on a circle.
3. Changes of rein in trot – out of the circle, across the short and long diagonals.
4. Frequent transitions between trot and walk.
5. Transitions between trot and canter on a circle (about every one or two circles).
6. Lengthening the stride (on the long side) – maintaining the tempo.
7. Allowing the horse to stretch down and chew the reins out of the rider's hands in rising trot.
8. One shallow loop on the long side.

The beginning of the training session: walking on a loose rein.

Circle work is valuable for improving flexion and bend.

9. Three-loop serpentines in rising trot with large, round loops.
10. Leg-yield to the outside (head to the wall).
11. Turns around the forehand.

All exercises and movements should be ridden on *the longest possible contact* (with poll flexion) to improve the horse's ability to work through the back.

After about half a year of training, more difficult exercises and movements can be introduced:

1. Frequent transitions between trot and canter on a circle (every half- or full circle).
2. Making the circle smaller (remaining on one track) and leg-yielding back out again.
3. Lengthening the steps on the open section of the circle. (The open section of, say, a 20 m circle started at A or C is the section that passes through X, i.e. that is not enclosed by the arena walls.)
4. Two shallow loops on the long side.
5. Leg-yield to the inside (head away from the wall).

Lengthening the stride in canter on the diagonal.

6. Riding 'squares' (figures with quarter-volte corners), making them smaller, then larger again.
7. Lengthening the stride on the long side, returning to the original stride length again on the short side.
8. Allowing the horse to stretch down into a longer contact, while chewing quietly at the bit in halt, walk, trot and canter.
9. Riding medium walk (on long reins to control poll flexion).

All exercises should be ridden first in walk, then trot then, when appropriate, canter. Suppleness of the back and flexibility through the ribs will be improved. A basic routine can be made up by choosing a number and sequence of different exercises and movements for the trainer/rider to follow, which can be adapted from horse to horse.

Collecting exercises in the second year

After the first year of training, work towards collection can begin. The following easy exercises are suitable for the young horse during the first month of this work:

1. Voltes in trot (large ones at first, of about 8 m in diameter).
2. Transitions from trot to halt and vice versa.
3. Turns around the haunches – haunches-in on a small half-circle.
4. Rein-back.
5. Medium trot and return to working stride length.
6. Canter from walk.
7. Voltes in canter (large ones at first, decreasing to about 8 m in diameter).
8. Lengthening the stride in canter and returning to working stride length.

In our experience, at the end of basic training for a 5- or 6-year-old horse, the following more difficult exercises relating to collection can be included:

1. Half-circles and returning to the track in a more collected trot, then resuming working trot.

2. Shoulder-fore, developing into shoulder-in on the long side.
3. Medium trot on the long side, collected trot on the short side.
4. Transitions from canter to walk, and vice versa.
5. Simple change of leg in canter with four or five walk steps (changing out of the circle or on the middle of the long side, or on the long or short diagonal).
6. Counter-canter.
7. Medium canter on the long side – collected canter on the short side.
8. Riding the exercises and movements with a double bridle with a 5½-year-old horse (sometimes earlier, sometimes later).

The sequence of exercises and movements is not compulsory but is variable from horse to horse. It is important, however, that the trainer/rider knows which exercise/movement suits each horse, in which order they should be ridden, and on which rein they should be executed in order to develop and improve working through the back and in relation to this looseness, rhythm, contact, impulsion, straightness and, with a 5-year-old horse, collection. Through this the horse will learn to take weight on his haunches.

It is always important to observe the suppleness and correct seat of the rider and the looseness of the horse's back. A great mistake, which affects future training, is to allow the horse's head to come behind the vertical and bend behind the poll, which causes the hind legs to trail behind the horse. With more collected exercises it is important to ride forwards in trot and canter to activate the hindquarters.

Practical experience

The most important aim at the beginning of a ridden session is *loosening up the horse.* It is only possible for a horse to remain in a correct outline with flowing movement while responding to the rider's aids if he is loose. Young horses have a natural length of frame in which they can remain supple while going forwards. The musculature of young horses, as with people, takes a long time to build up. This is why, in the first weeks of riding, the greater part of each training session consists of loosening exercises.

How do we progress with the young horse? Next, the reins are given

Circles or straight?

Strong and lively horses can be ridden earlier on a circle in order to quieten them. One rides lazy horses more easily on straight lines out hacking to encourage them to go forwards more willingly.

in walk. The rider sits quietly and waits for the horse to walk forward without rushing. A few cavalletti are a great help in encouraging the horse to stretch the neck forwards and down, freeing the back. The tail is sometimes clamped down at the beginning of exercises, but will slowly become freer as the musculature of the horse – especially in the back – becomes more relaxed.

When the horse comes out of the stable fresh and it is not possible to lunge him first, he cannot be loosened up properly in walk. One should then ride quietly in rising trot, controlling the forward movement of the horse sufficiently so that the driving aids can be used. Horses who already understand the rein aids quieten down more easily on a circle. The rider goes with the movement of the horse and quietens him down using the voice, looking ahead and keeping him in an even tempo and rhythm. The loosening-up phase should be at least 15–20 minutes with a young horse.

As training progresses the loosening-up phase becomes shorter so that we come more quickly to the work phase, but it must never be left out altogether. The aim of everyday riding with a youngster is to totally loosen the horse. There are riders who believe that an older horse does not need to be loosened up any more, and also that it is senseless to

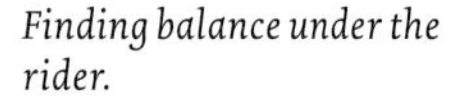

Finding balance under the rider.

ride out the exuberance that will later be needed for piaffe and passage, but the fact that they don't do so results in the horse going on his forehand. Such mistakes emerge when the system of training is not fully understood and one veers off the correct path. These errors show up in the horse who has not been properly loosened up as rhythm problems in walk, tense steps, tightness through the back and overbending with the head coming behind the vertical. A horse who has not been loosened up will be tense and all the muscle groups (especially in the back) that have not been warmed up become tight.

A fully loosened horse is able to use specific muscle groups for certain exercises, and relax them again, for example in medium walk or by the rider allowing the horse to stretch down into a longer contact, while chewing quietly at the bit. Real work begins only when the horse is loose enough.

Letting the horse look around him – every day there is something new!

The obedience of the horse to the rider's weight, leg and rein aids is tested in the dressage arena, when jumping or out hacking. As mentioned earlier, these are not separate subjects. This is why we build a complete programme for every hour during training. Always begin with easier exercises and gradually introduce more difficult ones.

It is unavoidable that we sometimes push the horse too hard; no trainer is perfect. However, experienced riders acknowledge that they are solely responsible for their mistakes. It is important to make the best of each situation. When we realize that our horses are being defensive and are not capable of giving any more, we must not resort to drastic measures. We must not lose sight of the future and lose the trust of the horse through him having bad experiences. Instead, by assessing the situation, ceasing the exercise and changing to another, easier one, we regain the horse's attention and restore his confidence, finishing on a good note.

It is often difficult to deal with young horses who take a long time to flex through the poll but meanwhile need the chance to stretch down into a longer contact in order to relax their neck muscles. We have discovered that, especially with young horses, a short rest every 10 or 15 minutes is beneficial. In this way certain problems, such as grabbing hold of the bit, can be avoided.

It is great when an exercise has been performed successfully and one can praise one's horse. The horse must always be rewarded for success

The day before is crucial

After a successful session, we can start where we left off on the following day.

whether the movement was easy or difficult, and this gives a good starting point for the next day. Basically, the horse should be rewarded for all exercises done well and ignored for the ones that were not.

The third part of the riding session comes under the heading riding in walk. As a general rule this means riding on a loose rein – which is unfortunately often neglected. For the rider it is simply a matter of being patient, but it is very important for the horse. A horse worked quietly in walk goes back calmly to his stable. It helps to restore an air of tranquillity, particularly if the horse has been rather excitable in his work. Also, developing a balanced, regular walk fluently ridden with big strides on loose reins is very important. We have always done this with both our dressage and eventing horses. About 5–10 minutes in walk is enough for the young horse, however hard he has been worked.

Controlling the working environment

We must never forget how important it is to regulate the other aspects of working a horse. Some riders have difficulty identifying when a horse is put under too much pressure during ridden work and over-exertion is not always obvious. Frisky and nervous horses can appear to be alert straight away but it takes time to loosen them up and finally ride them with driving aids. They can frequently spook. Some time after riding such horses we should visit them in the stable to check and reassure them. If they are standing listlessly they may be tired, in which case the training should be adjusted accordingly. Also, if a horse is still out of sorts an hour after being ridden, his temperature should be taken.

Horses can lose the desire to eat when changing from life in the field to the stable. The young horse can also have hooks on his teeth that prevent him chewing. Care of the young horse's teeth is therefore very important. However, the most important subject is care of the legs. Tendons and joints should be inspected regularly; if a horse has warm tendons or swollen joints these are often clear signs of overwork.

Do not forget

Riding quietly in walk at the end of a session and unwinding allows both horse and rider to begin with more motivation the next day.

An experienced groom who cares for the horse every day will notice such things and certainly feeling the legs should be part of the daily routine. However, the trainer may wish to do this personally for peace of mind and a responsible trainer will want to be aware on a daily basis of anything out of the ordinary.

To prevent leg problems it is a good idea to hose the legs after training (weather permitting) and to follow this with a brief massage. To do this one strokes a flat hand down the tendons and over the fetlock. In certain circumstances medicated ointment can be rubbed into the leg, after seeking advice from the vet.

One cannot be too careful with young horses and should not leave things until a problem occurs.

It goes without saying that regular care of the feet is most important. To prevent the hooves becoming brittle they should be greased after washing (not before riding). Working on good surfaces, it is perfectly possible for young horses to work unshod until their first competition, but the advice of the farrier should be taken regarding foot problems and keeping the feet trimmed at regular intervals. For jumping training and riding cross-country on grass, studs on the hind shoes are useful.

Finally, daily turnout in the paddock or field is very important. When the horse has a day off he should be allowed to relax in the field to keep him mentally healthy.

Stable management is just as important for the horse's well-being as the work in the school; Carmen Thiemann on feeding duty

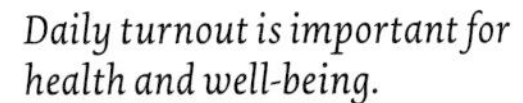

Daily turnout is important for health and well-being.

CHAPTER 4

Developing impulsion from suppleness

Learning the aids

Loosening up has already been covered in the previous chapter. Now we go on to discuss how the young horse comes to trust the rider's aids in order to develop impulsion. Apart from the voice, whip and spurs (although the last are not used in the initial stages of training), we are familiar with the weight, leg and rein aids. To help the young horse develop further his understanding of the rider's aids there are certain exercises ridden on the bit that are useful. Riding theses exercises can improve obedience to individual aids, as well as improving the way the horse works overall, for example when riding the movements required at Novice-level dressage. Further specialized dressage training follows the required movements at Elementary, Medium and Advanced levels. Every successive level requires a certain standard of training which takes about one year to achieve. Throughout basic training, movements should be consolidated to ensure that the horse understands them before progressing further.

The horse's natural ability should be developed with gymnastic training. We want to make the horse more beautiful and improve his condition. We want to train using the art of dressage, and not by teaching tricks in the arena.

One cannot be warned enough about the dangers of spoiling the gaits through taking short cuts in training. Unfortunately we see a large number of competition horses who, by performing poor exercises just to make them obedient, have lost the expression of movement. The danger of such developments is that the horse does not work correctly on the bit. Because of the dramatic growth in the number of competitors, perhaps the dressage tests should be shortened, which would place more emphasis on the ability to perform a sequence of movements (transitions and changes of direction, etc.) in quick succession.

Exercises

Exercises are the means to the end and should not be ridden just for the sake of it.

A lovely working trot with a light contact.

More emphasis is already placed upon the clarity of the gaits at the lower levels.

Obedience to the forward-driving aids

We continue with the training of the young horse. Now, when the young horse is relaxed and ready to proceed after loosening up, the driving aids need to be developed further. The lower leg is placed more firmly in position and driving can be helped by use of the voice. Once the horse reacts he should be rewarded immediately. If he does not react, the aids must be firmer.

Through repetition of the voice/leg aids supported, when necessary, with a whip aid, we want to reach the stage where the young horse will respond purely to the leg aid. We will not then need to use the voice or whip anymore, except on those occasions when he does not react of his own accord to leg pressure.

Response to the driving aids is absolutely necessary for the development of the carrying power of the haunches. It is not achieved in any other way. However, the ability of the hind legs to take weight cannot be achieved just by driving; the support of the reins in the rider's hands is also required, that is a steady contact.

In order for the horse to develop his individual length of stride and power he must work on the bit, flexing at the poll and being in the required outline for the stage of training. A good test of whether the training has been correct is to lengthen the steps two or three times on the long sides of the arena at the end of the training session.

Establishing a contact (use of the poll)

Establishing a contact can be viewed as a progressive process:

- Riding with a contact between the rider's hands and the horse's mouth without flexion at the poll, for example with young horses when first sitting in the saddle (for safety reasons).
- Riding on long reins; the longest, lightest contact between the rider's hands and the horse's mouth where the horse flexes through the poll. This is important in medium walk and also at the beginning of the ridden session if the horse has over-developed muscles on the underside of the neck or problems in the poll.

A soft contact develops feel.

- Riding on the bit (where the reins are shorter by 7–8 cm than when riding on long reins), which alters the outline of the neck to that required when riding collected walk, trot and canter. (The horse must be able to do this in a snaffle before being introduced to a double bridle later in his training.)

Riding with loose reins, that is, riding on the buckle at the beginning and end of a riding session, relinquishes the contact and allows the horse to stretch.

The question of how we ride the horse on the bit cannot be answered fully in a couple of sentences. It is not simply a matter of shortening the reins and keeping a contact with the horse's mouth. The horse must understand what his correct reaction to the reins being taken up should be: he simply remains in the required outline without resistance; without grabbing the bit or throwing his head about. To achieve this, the rein aids can only be used in co-ordination with bracing the lower back (weight aids) and leg aids (half-halts).

Up to now the horse has been ridden with giving hands to encourage the suppleness of his neck when stretching forwards and

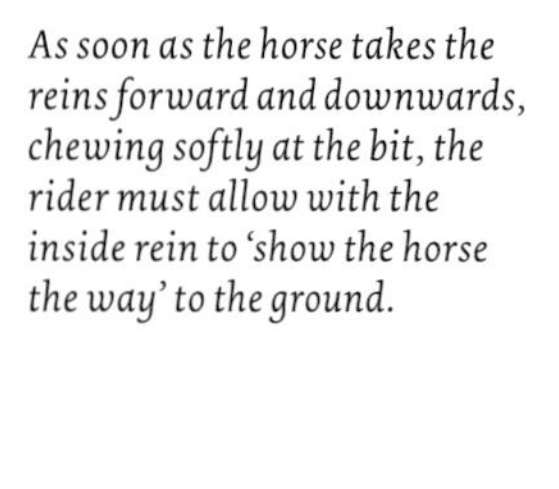

As soon as the horse takes the reins forward and downwards, chewing softly at the bit, the rider must allow with the inside rein to 'show the horse the way' to the ground.

down, but there comes the point in the first stage of training when the rider can feel the horse take a contact. With driving aids the horse is asked to take fluent steps in trot. The rider's hands contain the impulsion. The contact in the hand should be just sufficient to allow the horse to work from his hindquarters, with a supple back, fluid impulsion and flexion through the poll.

This requires a lot of 'feel' on behalf of the rider. From the beginning the rider must be aware of working the horse too strongly into a contact as this would cause tension. Instead, a contact must be maintained that is as light as possible with the horse's mouth, with soft, feeling hands. Flexible elbows and shoulders are absolutely essential to having correctly still hands.

The required outline is produced by using half-halts and by working into a contact so that the horse steps confidently to the bit, flexing at the poll. The development of the carrying power of the haunches is influenced by how the neck is set on, and its conformation. The horse should carry his neck forwards (that is, it should not be contracted); this will give the rider the feeling of having 'more horse in front'. The carrying power of the horse has to be developed further with appropriate work. For example, medium trot on the long sides is prepared for by riding three or four steps in the corner in shorter strides in order to take more weight onto the hind legs first. At the next corner, this exercise is repeated with more engagement.

In this way the strength of the horse is developed and movement is channelled forwards through a swinging back, requiring the full concentration of the rider to ride the horse 'from back to front' and not the other way around. Necks that are pulled in inhibit the building of the back muscles and hinder the natural movement of the horse. The exact opposite of this is only achievable by a correctly trained rider. We would remind you, while on this subject, that softness is required for successful training. If a horse's neck is forced into an outline too soon, the rider is already on the wrong track and can cause injury. 'Tight in the neck', 'behind the vertical', 'mouth problems', 'tight in the back', 'tense movement', 'problems with rhythm', 'shortening of the strides' and 'changes in temperament' are all defects unfortunately caused by trying to force improvements in neck carriage, which may include the unnecessary use of draw-reins.

The mystery of effectiveness

The mystery of the effectiveness of the rider is to establish softness in the horse with 'feel', energy and co-ordination of the weight, leg and rein aids which remain invisible to the observer.

1

2

1 *Here everything is correct: the horse's enjoyment of his work shows in his expression.*

2 *This horse has an unhappy expression; this outline causes the horse discomfort..*

In the first stage of training we try to ensure that the horse is obedient to the forward-driving and lateral aids of the rider. Thus the horse learns to obey the aids and it is up to the rider to influence and develop the gaits, straightness, and bending.

The development of the aids is part of the rider's training. The rider should learn this on an older, experienced horse. Without sufficient experience on the rider's part, there is a great risk of problems occurring throughout the horse's training. Every single exercise must be learned and it must be understood how it teaches the driving and collecting aids.

A rider with limited experience who wants to buy a young horse should at least buy one who has already been ridden and on whom time and money has already been spent. With luck, the rider should have the opportunity to ride a variety of other horses, which helps in learning the application of the aids. In this way, many rider problems can be avoided and training can begin with a solid foundation.

The right combination

A young rider belongs on an experienced horse, and an experienced rider on a young horse.

Obedience to the aids for lateral movement

We have already discussed the forward-driving aids (weight and leg aids) and their use in such actions as moving off from halt, or into trot. We have also seen how the rider has used the first collecting aids to place the horse 'on the bit' with half-halts. Next in this stage of training we concentrate on developing and improving the response to the aids that ask for a degree of sideways movement in one direction.

Turn on the forehand

An important exercise which helps the young horse to understand one-sided, lateral-driving and supporting aids is the turn on the forehand. This can be described as a loosening exercise (useful in a rest period between trot exercises), which helps to develop response to the weight aids, the lateral-driving and supporting leg aids, and individual rein aids.

The horse is halted, for example, on the left rein on the inner track of the school. The rider sits with more weight on the right seat bone (without collapsing the hip) and shortens the right rein while slightly softening the outside (left) rein. (Note that the terms 'inside' and 'outside' refer in all circumstances to the bend of the horse and not to the layout of the arena, or the horse's position in it.) The first reaction must be that the horse softens to the bit when he feels the contact with the right rein. When he does this, he must be rewarded with the voice, otherwise the rein should be shortened a little more. Next, the rider places the inside (right) leg slightly behind the girth and more firmly on the horse and pushes the hindquarters around the forehand step by step, with the hind legs crossing until the turn is complete. If the horse does not respond to the leg aid, then the whip can be used just behind the right leg. As an additional aid, feeling softly on the inside (right) rein can ask the neck and head to bend inwards slightly.

The outside (left) leg lies further behind the girth and controls the hindquarters step by step as they turn. If the turn becomes too hurried, it may be best to use the inside (right) leg aid every other step when the inside hind leg steps across and the outside hind leg is still. The inside leg aid can also be useful to prevent the horse from stepping backwards. Once the exercise is successful the horse should have a break and be rewarded.

If the young horse has his introduction to the lateral-driving aids in this way, we can ensure that he works in other exercises from the inside weight aid into the outside rein. The one-sided bracing of the rider's lower back is important to prevent the horse stepping backwards, which is a fault. The outside (left) rein has a double function: it prevents the horse falling out through his outside shoulder, which is a slight fault, and prevents him from stepping forwards (a bigger fault). At this point, we should explain that the turn on the forehand can be

Leg-yielding in walk familiarizes the horse with the lateral-driving aids.

A more advanced level of work: lateral work in trot.

used as a correction, with horses who ignore the inside leg aid, for example, which is often a result of poorly given leg aids by the rider.

In addition to its role in training the horse, by riding the turn on the forehand a novice rider learns the effect of the inside and outside legs and also how to place their weight as an aid.

Turn on the forehand is, then, important in the training of the young horse and the novice rider, and it is not used often enough. Later, the turn on the forehand will be used as a preparation for rein-back. Horses who are obstinate when asked to step backwards can find it easier when they are asked to perform a turn on the forehand first.

Leg-yielding

Leg-yielding belongs with the loosening exercises whereby the horse becomes familiar with the rider's forward- and lateral-driving aids (and is also described as a preparatory exercise). Leg-yielding is ridden first in walk and later in (a shortened) working trot. It should only be used for short periods.

With the horse on the right rein, leg-yielding with the horse facing *towards the wall* is asked for as follows: the rider's weight is placed on the left seat bone, with the left (inside) leg near or slightly behind the girth asking the horse to move his body away from the wall at an angle of between 35 and 45 degrees to the track. The left leg should be used at the moment the left hind foot leaves the ground, making it easier for the horse to step forwards/sideways and cross his legs. The right (outside) leg is placed further back than the inside leg to prevent the horse from travelling sideways too much.

The left rein (inside rein in relation to the bend of the horse) asks for flexion and the right (outside) rein supports the outside shoulder and prevents the horse bending his neck too much.

If the horse bends his neck rather than correctly bending around the rider's inside leg, the correct bend through his body should be established by riding different exercises such as a small volte through each corner of a square, or by riding each corner as a leg-yield facing inwards, making sure that the outside rein prevents too much neck bend.

Riding leg-yield facing *away from the wall* around the arena has great value as a training exercise in preparation for shoulder-fore and shoulder-in. It accustoms the horse to stepping away from the rider's inside leg into the outside rein. In leg-yielding the horse moves sideways by crossing his fore and hind legs on two separate tracks with less bend through his body than is required for shoulder-fore (where the horse moves on four narrow tracks) and shoulder-in (where, in the form required for competition dressage, the horse moves on three distinct tracks). The angle ridden in leg-yielding depends on the ability of the horse. A smaller angle is easier as it requires less crossing of the horse's legs. A greater angle of approaching 45 degrees to the wall is quite demanding and requires a great amount of crossing of the legs.

Shallow loops in leg-yield

To develop the forward-lateral driving weight and leg aids further, shallow loops in leg-yield can be ridden. The horse moves laterally as in leg-yield, moving further to the inside of the arena as he steps away from the corner. The more secure the horse is on the outside aids (the right side aids when stepping to the right) the less the flexion can be.

The size of the loops depends on the horse's level of training. As a general rule the centre point of the loop where the flexion changes

1

2

1 *Leg-yielding inwards on a shallow loop . . .*

2 *. . . and out again.*

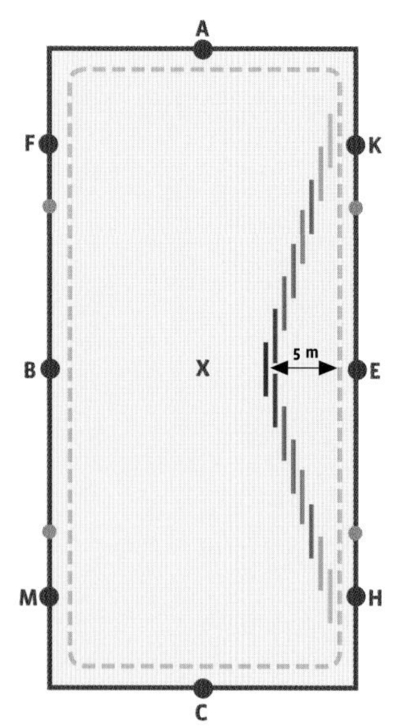

Riding a shallow loop in leg-yield.

should be 5 m in from the track, and it should be ridden with sufficient flexion so that it finishes at a corresponding point on the track to where it began (for example, if it began at the H quarter marker, it should finish at K). At first, however, only a few steps will be possible. Once these are successful, the lateral steps can be maintained from the first quarter marker to X. The inner hind foot must step further forward so that the suppleness and ability to work through the back in walk, and even more so in trot, is improved.

To ride the exercise the rider needs to give the following aids. After riding through a corner on the left rein the rider flexes the horse slightly to the right, puts more weight onto the right seat bone and takes the lower legs back – the outside (left leg) more so. At the starting point the right (now the inside) leg gives the aid to move the horse forwards and laterally towards the middle of the arena. The horse is kept parallel to the wall. The rider's left leg is used to support the horse and, when necessary, to control the forward movement. When the changeover point is reached, the horse should be ridden straight for one horse's length and flexed in the new direction. He should be ridden back to the track in the same way. Once he reaches the track, the exercise is complete.

Riding on curved lines

Having established the turn on the forehand and leg-yielding the horse should work better on each rein and react better to our individual aids, so we can now concentrate on riding correctly on curved lines. The requirements of doing so correctly at Novice level include circles, serpentines, riding correctly through corners (a half-10 m circle comes next), a half-volte and return to the track, riding on a circle with longer steps on the open section (away from the wall), or a figure of eight on the short side, with circles 10 m in diameter. All exercises should be ridden first in walk, and then later in trot and canter (with changes of lead, where appropriate, through trot or walk).

We are familiar with the meaning of flexion (flexing the head to the inside) from the loosening exercises. With flexion, which occurs only at the poll, one should see the horse's inside eye and nostril; the crest of the mane should not twist to the inside. Bending (through the whole

Is training successful so far?

The young horse is being trained correctly if he can remain in self-carriage and secure in his rhythm on both reins by the end of his first year's training.

length of the horse) is only possible when the horse is able to collect and carry weight on his haunches. The bend is initiated in the area of the ribs, around the rider's inside leg, but extends through the whole horse from head to tail. For example, in an 8 m volte to the left the horse is both flexed to the left and bent so that he is 'straight' on the track of the circle, that is, his hind feet follow precisely the tracks of his forefeet.

The outside rein controls the amount of flexion and bend.

Riding turns

Up till now the young horse has not learned to bend through his body but we can begin to develop collection by riding turns. Turns should be ridden as large curves without preventing the horse from stepping forwards under his body and maintaining the rhythm. Once the horse can soften and responds to slight inside aids we can begin to ask for a greater degree of bend in which the outside hind leg steps under more.

How do we ask for bending (for example, riding a corner)? On a curve the outside pair of legs follow a longer track than the inside legs. The inside rein leads the horse into the turn and the inside leg, near the girth, keeps the horse going forwards. The outside rein must give a little to allow the horse to bend, without losing the contact necessary

This rider is correctly positioning the horse to the right.

Flexion and bending

A flexed horse is not always bent; but a bent horse is always flexed.

to prevent the horse from falling out through his outside shoulder. A firm outside leg aid is also required for this purpose. One must not forget to soften the inside rein at the earliest opportunity so that the horse does not lean on it or come behind the vertical.

Every turn also involves a combination of weight aids, applied by stepping into the inside stirrup and taking more weight on the inside seat bone. The outside shoulder is brought forwards so that the rider's shoulders remain parallel to those of the horse.

Riding a turn.

When an increased amount of bending is asked for, young horses can either fall in, or step to the inside with the inside hind leg. Both situations must be prevented by firmer aids with the outside rein and inside leg. With a trained horse, a corner should be ridden as a quarter volte of about 6 m in diameter. A young horse would find this too difficult, so the corners should be based on figures of 8 or 10 m in diameter.

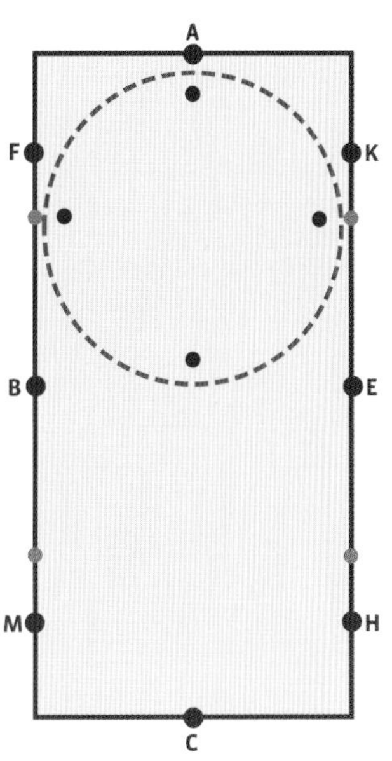

Cones are useful for marking out a correct circle, as well as other school movements.

Riding on a circle

Earlier, we discussed using circles to calm down fresh or nervous horses. Here, we are looking at their gymnastic value. Riding a circle involves riding a horse on a continuous bend and we have to consider the natural crookedness of the horse, which is discussed further at the start of Chapter 5. As with corners, it is easier for the horse if the circle is large. With very young horses, cones can be used to mark out four equidistant points (about 2 m in from the circumference) to make it easier for the horse to trot on a circle.

Horses who have not learned this exercise on the lunge (and many riders) may find it difficult to produce an evenly round circle in which the horse neither falls out through the outside shoulder nor falls in on the open section of the circle.

Besides simple circles, other bending exercises based on them include 10 m voltes, a half-volte and returning to the track or a figure of eight on the short side produced by riding two 10 m circles.

Riding loops and serpentines

Riding loops and serpentines is a good way to familiarize the young horse further with the weight, seat and leg aids for turning, as described earlier. Riders should be familiar with these figures. A single shallow loop on the long side of the arena should be 5 m in depth and ridden from corner marker to corner marker, and a double loop should have two loops 2.5 m deep and touch the track between the loops at the halfway marker. We begin by riding a single shallow loop; it is best to walk the exercise first to make sure that the horse understands it before proceeding in trot.

Single and double loops on the long sides.

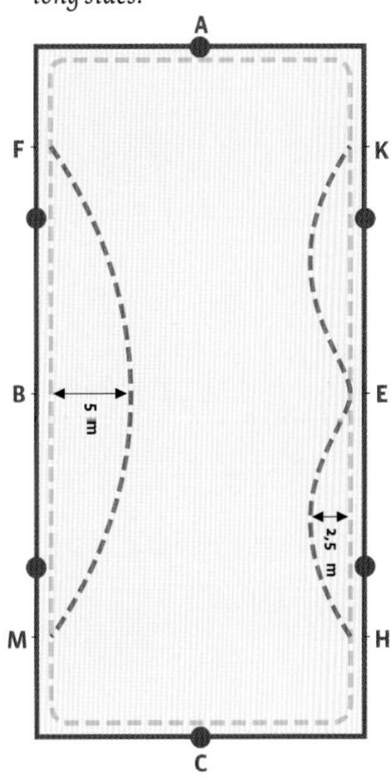

Serpentines are important for developing suppleness in the young horse. This will have many benefits as training progresses, not only for

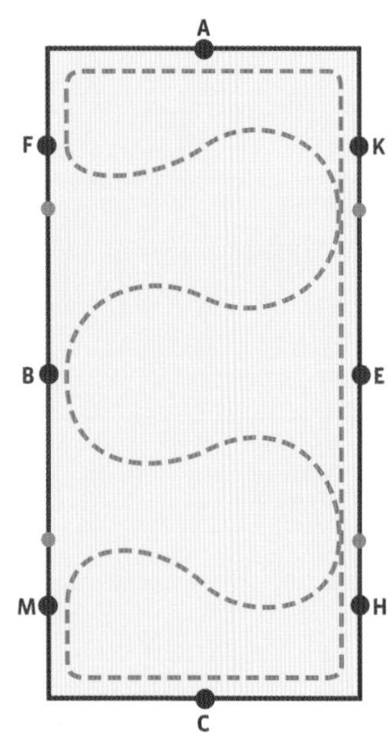

A good 'old-fashioned' serpentine is an extremely valuable gymnastic exercise to improve flexion, bending and turning.

dressage but also for activities such as showjumping and cross-country. It is usual to start with a three-loop serpentine across the whole arena (ridden first in rising trot), building up to four and five loops later on.

(It is hard to understand why some trainers insist on riding serpentines that are straight across the centre line. It is much better for young horses, ridden by experienced riders, to perform serpentines as they used to be, on curved lines with a change of bend over the centre line.)

Serpentines help the inexperienced rider to develop the aids with the inside leg, and to learn how to improve flexion by softening the horse with the inside rein. The young horse also learns these aids and becomes more flexible through the ribs as a result. When progressing to serpentines of four or more loops, these should be ridden in sitting trot to keep the horse more secure in the contact (flexion through the poll). Flexion requires a slightly shorter inside rein, and requires the outside rein to give slightly in order to keep the contact even by following the line of the bend. The new outside rein on each loop is controlled by the rider's elbow and wrist.

A figure of eight on the short side – plastic blocks ensure accurate riding.

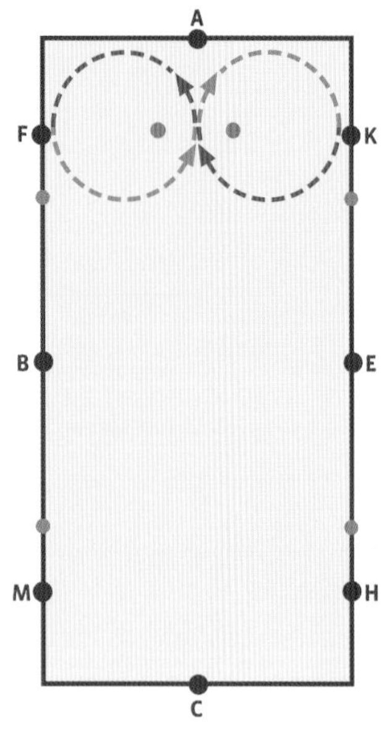

Voltes and the figure of eight

Once a young horse can be ridden on serpentines, bending exercises can be developed further by introducing large voltes and figures of eight (see diagram). Voltes are ridden in a similar manner to 10 m loops in a serpentine. We try to ride each corner of the arena in this way; here, it is easier to control the outside shoulder of the horse and make sure that the figure is ridden on one track. A figure of eight can be asked for when consecutive corners are ridden as part of a 10 m volte on each rein. The horse is flexed the same as when riding serpentines. Five or six figures of eight can be ridden in the training session (beginning in walk so that the horse understands the exercise) before finishing by lengthening the steps on the long side (first in rising trot, then later in sitting) to freshen the tempo. Riding figures of eight improves contact, working through the back, suppleness and response to the rider's seat and inside aids. This is one of the most difficult, yet most effective exercises. Do not forget to ride the horse energetically forwards afterwards, though.

1

2

3

4

1–2 *Riding a figure of eight.*

3–4 *A good example of flexion and bend, riding a volte to the left.*

Full and half-halts

The horse should now be able to be ridden forwards in trot and obedient to the forward-driving aids. He should understand the turn on the forehand, leg-yielding and working on curved lines, and respond to the lateral-driving (individual) aids. We are now at the most difficult stage of basic training, that is, using exercises that confirm a correct contact with the mouth and establish the horse on the bit. This work is primarily achieved with half-halts; the rider's hand must remain passive and quietly keep the head and neck in a steady outline (with flexion at the poll). Now we can go a step further and ask the horse to work more through his back.

The key exercise is the halt. This is both the test of a horse working through his back while maintaining his outline, and being able to shorten and lengthen his stride without resistance, or any disturbance in his movement or rhythm.

In the full halt the horse is brought to a standstill by way of one or more half-halts (which requires the horse to work through his back and a rider who understands the aids) from any gait. However, half-halts are also the means to change gait, regulate the tempo within a gait and shorten the stride. These are used to develop training further, by maintaining the rhythm and the outline of the horse and with the aim of improving the gaits (the start of collection).

The half-halt

Half-halts are used frequently. They should be given by the rider before every new exercise or movement, for example before changing direction, or changing the tempo. A half-halt is used to keep the horse's attention in the same way as the command 'listen!' would be used, as mentioned by Müseler in his book *Riding Logic*.

The half-halt has the function of asking the hindquarters to engage more in order to carry more weight whilst the horse maintains flexion at the poll.

How do we ask a young horse for half-halts? Certainly not by pulling on the reins. The aids are a combination of weight, leg and rein aids. The rider braces the lower back and drives the horse with even leg aids on both sides into a steady contact. In this moment the rider (for

Half-halts are given to:

- Regulate the tempo and shorten the gaits.
- Control the outline.
- Prepare before starting a new exercise/movement.
- Achieve, maintain and improve collection.

example in trot) keeps the contact equal in both hands, and then instantly softens the inside rein. This encourages the horse to take more weight on his hind legs and (in canter, for example) to lower his haunches. This the ideal scenario. At an earlier stage of training, half-halts have to be given somewhat more obviously and frequently.

A simple example of a half-halt is to ride transitions from trot to walk and vice versa, and a more difficult exercise is from canter to walk, and walk to canter without any trot steps. The aim of this training is that *the aids must be always clear to the horse, and almost invisible to the onlooker.*

Half-halts are the mystery of classical riding

The more frequently, sensitively and invisibly the rider can give half-halts, the more easily the horse will learn to take weight behind, becoming lighter on his feet and more flexible in his movement.

With young horses the reaction to the half-halt can be reinforced by the voice. It takes a long time for a horse to properly understand and accept half-halts and it is impossible to say that these will be fully developed in a short space of time. The rider needs the experience and feel in order to establish the precise aiding required for half-halts. Driving too strongly with the weight and leg aids brings the horse too strongly into the reins so that the brief moment of giving the rein is passed by and he ends up pulling against the bit. Should the horse have no respect for the driving aids or the giving of the inside rein, and tries to lean on the bit, this is best corrected on the circle with new application of the aids.

It is important that the horse is given no support from the reins should he try to lean against them. The rider must have quick reactions in order to correct this. It is necessary to vary the contact between holding and giving and at the same time support the horse with the weight and leg aids to limit the resistance. After a short interval the aids should be re-applied and the horse rewarded once they are successful (especially with young horses) in order to achieve a light and easy response. The horse will then thank us again for being patient. One of the mysteries in dealing with horses is their readiness to try to follow the rider's aids when they are not prepared enough or asked at the right time. Over time, the lighter the half-halts given, the greater influence the rider has over the horse, which results in harmony between rider and horse.

The correct procedure

'First give then take', our old riding instructor Major a.D.Paul Stecken always said. 'No rider must forget that he has taken up the contact.' How right he was!

It is most important to maintain a soft wrist. With progressive training the bracing of the back and a light flexion of the wrist are enough to ask for a half-halt that is barely visible to the observer, who

1

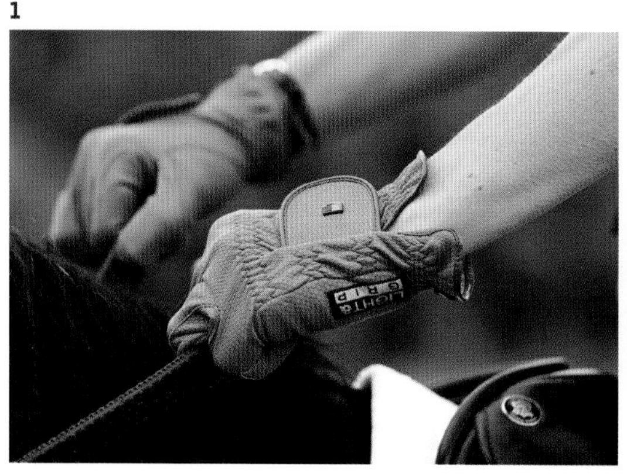

2

1 *This is not allowed!*

2 *A correct hand position guarantees a feeling contact with the reins.*

simply sees a change in the overall picture of the horse – improvement of the outline, tempo, gaits, etc. It is then that riding becomes an art.

One way to establish a quiet and correct hand position is to bridge the reins. For this, both reins pass through each hand and are held evenly. In jumping and cross-country riding this also gives security should the rider be thrown forwards onto the horse's neck.

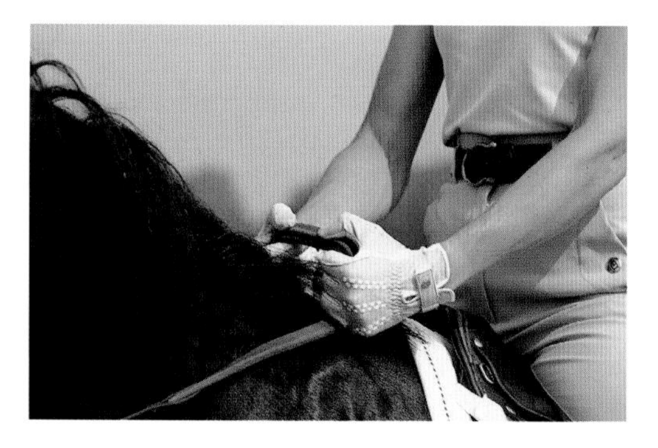

Bridging the reins is one way to improve the hand position and to control the use of the reins.

The full halt

In the first year of training full halts are practised from walk and trot. To begin with, halt should be asked for on the track, using the wall as a support and guide to keep the horse straight.

The halt is prepared with one or more half-halts. The number of half-halts depends on how well the horse works through his back and the ability of the rider to ask for them. Once the horse comes to halt, the rider must make sure that he stands still with his weight evenly

If a young horse cannot stand absolutely square, this is an indication that his basic training needs more attention.

placed on all four legs. The rider sits upright and prevents the hind legs from stepping back with the weight and leg aids and can correct the horse should he leave one (or both) hind legs out behind. As soon as the halt is correct the rider's hands give forwards to relax the horse's neck, but maintain a light contact with the mouth to keep the head and neck steady and maintain flexion at the poll.

If the horse does not stand square, the earlier stages of training should be improved. The horse should be allowed to walk one or two steps forwards into halt in the beginning. When one hind leg is always out behind, the horse should be asked to step forwards with it to square up the halt. The exercise is successful when halt can be asked for at specific markers. Basically, the horse should be taught to stand still and square for a minimum of four to five seconds (the length of time it takes to salute, or to halt before asking for rein-back, turn on the haunches, etc).

1

2

1 *Taking weight behind in preparation for halt.*

2 *Standing square.*

Rein-back

Rein-back is an exercise in which the horse steps backwards in a footfall of diagonal pairs, as in trot. It is not normally ridden in the first year of training, but at the beginning of the second year when the young horse can make full halts easily from walk and trot. It is too soon to ask for rein-back when a horse has not learned to take weight behind through halting correctly.

Rein-back can be described as having two equal functions. It improves the horse's ability to work through the back (although it requires a degree of ability to do this before it can be attempted), and develops collection. It is a movement the horse rarely performs in nature, and one must take care that he does not perceive it as a punishment. This does not mean that a young horse cannot go backwards – some young horses will try to avoid the rider's aids by creeping back (although this is not desirable and does not constitute correct rein-back.) In normal cases, however, young horses try to evade by running forwards rather than going back.

Not backwards, only forwards

Rein-back begins with the driving aids, and then the rein aids are applied.

Which aids should we give to teach the young horse to rein-back? We need a combination of weight, leg and rein aids. The starting point

1

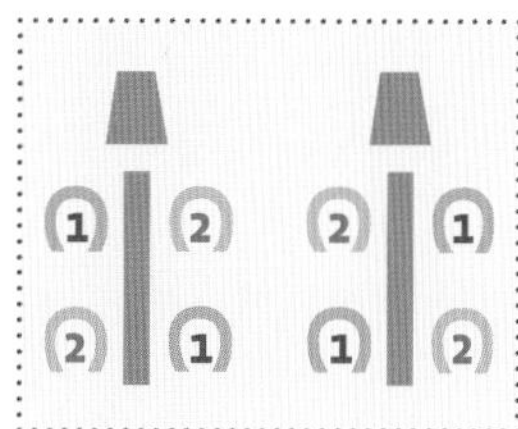

The sequence of steps in rein-back.

2

1 *Standing still in a square halt in preparation for rein-back.*

2 *Stepping backwards in diagonal pairs. The rider's legs are placed behind the girth.*

is a horse who is straight, steady in the contact and can halt square. We then give essentially the same aids with the weight and legs as to go forwards, although at the beginning of the rein-back the rider's legs are placed back behind the girth to correct any crookedness of the steps.

The rein contact is held in the same moment as the horse goes to step forwards, which starts the steps backwards in diagonal pairs. Once the rein-back commences the leg aids should be lightened to prevent the horse from going backwards too fast, and the rein aids can also be softened.

For young horses and those with hollow backs, rein-back can be made easier by the rider not sitting too strongly on the horse's back, and leaning slightly forwards with the upper body. The first driving aids for the rein-back must come from the legs.

With horses who have difficulty understanding the aids for rein-back and lock the poll we try to follow this method: in the moment that the horse lifts his inside hind foot, we take up the rein on the same side. Should the rein-back become crooked or resistant, it is easier to ask the horse to step onto the leg that is already behind (by using the leg aid on the same side) as it is carrying less weight and is the easiest leg for the horse to move. Asking him to move the leg that is more forward (carrying more weight) requires greater effort and can cause him to raise his head and tighten his back in his effort to move backwards.

When a horse has been rewarded for a successful rein-back, the movement must not be used as a punishment in the future. When a horse resists against the rein-back a helper may be needed to tap the forelegs with a schooling whip to start the backward movement. While this can work well, it may also cause more resistance. The best alternative is for the rider to dismount and tap the front legs with the whip personally, rewarding the horse when he understands.

In training, a horse should not be asked to go backwards for more than a horse's length otherwise this will increase the likelihood that he will think it is a punishment. A horse's length is three to four steps.

Test: trot – halt – rein-back – halt – trot

The following is a useful exercise. Halt from trot and stand square and still for four or five seconds, having prepared the horse with half-halts to maintain a softly flexed poll and elastic contact. Place the legs slightly back to ask for a straight rein-back and after three or four steps half-halt before taking a step forwards. Halt for four to five seconds, and then proceed in trot without any walk steps!

Four steps should be aimed for, to make the movement clear; two steps are not enough. After completing the rein-back, a square halt must be established. Should the horse leave a hind leg out behind, he should be asked to take one step forwards with it to correct the halt.

We must not forget that exercises are the means to the end, and not done just for the sake of it. As described earlier, we need rein-back to develop the horse's ability to work through the back and improve collection.

CHAPTER 5

The basic gaits: assessment and improvement

Riding straight – the natural crookedness of the horse

Although the fundamental part of straightness is developed in the second year of training it should have already been a significant part of training in the first year. In this chapter, straightness is covered in more detail.

We have patiently loosened the young horse, established regularity in his gaits and asked him to go in a regular rhythm. The development of the horse has been improved by his reaction to the forward- and lateral-driving aids and the collecting aids. As training progresses there will be a few issues to resolve along the way, for example further improving looseness to optimize the development of the gaits. In order to ride forwards with true impulsion we must ensure the straightness of the horse. The horse's hind feet should follow precisely the tracks of his forefeet on both straight and curved lines. A good way to improve straightness, lengthen the steps and improve cadence is to ride on curved lines, especially rounded serpentines.

The *natural crookedness* of the horse stems more or less from birth. In many cases this is shown, for example, by the right hind leg stepping out to the right rather than into the right fore hoofprint. The horse is most commonly crooked from the right hind leg to the left foreleg. This means that the horse goes against the rider's right leg and does not want to take a contact with the right rein. He tries to lean on the left rein and fall out with the left shoulder. Such a horse naturally finds left canter easier as the left hind leg can take more weight more easily, which then causes it to become more developed than the right hind leg. For this reason horses often go cross-country and over a course of jumps on the left lead. With those horses who are crooked the other way, everything is reversed.

Lengthening the stride improves suppleness.

On the right rein, the rider leads the forehand to the right with the right rein to bring the right foreleg onto the same track as the right hind leg. The rider's right leg lies slightly behind the girth and works with a forwards/sideways influence to drive the escaping right hind leg to the left. The rider's left leg gives a forward-driving aid at the girth and controls the flow of the movement. The left hand maintains the contact and prevents the horse from falling out through the outside shoulder. This exercise is a hint of shoulder-fore to the right, where the horse should not lean on the outside rein.

How do we recognize the natural crookedness of the horse and make him straight? We should understand that the natural crookedness of the horse is improved very little by attempting to ride on straight lines. He will only go straight on a straight line at this stage if the hind legs are not yet taking his weight.

In our experience natural crookedness is eliminated only by systematic schooling using serpentines, lengthening the stride on the open section of the circle and riding figures of eight to improve suppleness on both sides of the horse. When we are training our horses they respond best with the following principles: we drive with the inside aids into the outside supporting aids on a circle and on all curved lines. For example, in working trot on a circle left, the left (inside) leg drives the horse into the quietly supportive outside rein, so the horse takes the contact and therefore softens to the inside rein. The horse often snorts when he is loosened and softened in this way.

It can happen that the horse feels stiff to ride the day after a session which included many serpentines and circles. The muscles are unused to this new work and can ache, but this will pass after a couple of days (this is nothing to worry about; the trainer is doing a good job). The horse will gradually become straighter on the left rein once we achieve a contact with the right (outside) rein. The same goes on the right rein for when the left rein is the outside rein. A softly giving inside rein ensures a contact with the outside rein, enabling the horse to be ridden forwards.

A similar exercise in further training is shoulder-in, or the milder version which we call shoulder-fore. Here, for example on the long side of the arena on the left rein, the horse's neck is slightly flexed to the inside (left). The rider's inside (left) hand gives slightly so that the contact is not tight, thus preventing the horse from coming behind the vertical. The outside (right) hand remains quietly in place. In this way the contact with the outside (right) rein is improved, together with the straightness. We use the shoulder-fore exercise to develop the connection between the inside hind leg and the outside rein. To achieve this, the forehand is brought slightly to the inside – sometimes termed riding 'in position' – a posture that will later be developed into shoulder-in on three tracks.

A more advanced exercise is *leg-yielding in trot on the open section of the circle*, which improves the connection between the rider's inside leg and outside rein even more.

When we can keep the horse straight with our aids when working on circles and straight lines we have made significant progress. Improved bending can be achieved by riding curved lines with precision, so the inside hind leg takes more weight. The amount of weight taken can be improved by the exercise spiralling in on a circle onto a 10 m volte (on one track). We should ride this only for a short time before leg-yielding out again onto a large circle, and then ride some lengthened strides on the long side to maintain the rhythm and tempo. Another alternative way of riding out of the volte is to increase the circle on one track, finishing in rising trot (to release the horse's back) to freshen the tempo. One should work out which exercise is most suitable for each individual horse.

Always ride forwards to keep the movement powerful and the contact secure.

The natural crookedness of the horse can become apparent when riding lateral steps on the open side of a circle.

The exercise of spiralling in on a circle on one track and leg-yielding back out is a difficult loosening exercise. It can often be confused with a simpler exercise of just making the circle smaller and larger. The loading of the inside hind leg is increased very quickly if this is used as a collecting exercise by riding travers when making the circle smaller and shoulder-in when making it larger.

We must always keep an eye on the improvement of the energy and quality of the trot. We especially want the horse to go straight forwards with increased engagement. There should be no resistance when working on circles and curved lines, the aim being to improve the movement of the horse and produce impulsion by using the inside driving aids into the outside supporting aids (inside seat bone and inside leg into the outside rein and outside leg without collapsing at the hip). It is important to notice even the slightest error, otherwise the horse ends up crooked.

If the horse becomes crooked when going forwards on straight lines, it can be beneficial to ride exercises such as circles, serpentines and figures of eight to re-establish the straightness, i.e. the hind feet must step in the tracks of the forefeet. Once this is achieved on curved lines, the horse should be ridden straight forwards again, lengthening the steps to refresh the rhythm and tempo. When riding straight forwards on the left rein the right hind leg is prevented from escaping (to avoid stepping under) by riding alongside the wall. Rising trot makes it easier for the horse to swing through from behind.

An example of correcting crookedness in canter is as follows: a horse who brings his haunches in on the long side is flexed more to the inside through the corner, as in shoulder-in, and then driven forward. This activates the hind legs and encourages them to spring forward under the horse and take more weight.

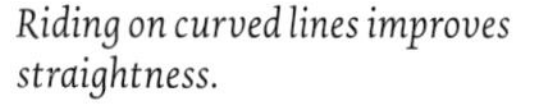

Riding on curved lines improves straightness.

Improving the basic gaits

After about a year the horse should be loose, have a good rhythm and work into a steady contact; he should be fairly straight and his natural impulsion is developing by working through his back, leading towards collection. We have thus achieved the requirements for continuing on to the next stage of training: there should be nothing in the way of progress except for the natural ability of the horse. On this issue, we must not make assumptions too readily. Certainly, an experienced trainer can tell a good horse by seeing him running free, and assess his individual qualities and future possibilities but, although there are horses who are ridden well and whose basic gaits are rated highly, not every horse is able to get good marks in all three gaits. This is dependent on conformation and the individual character of the horse. However, by using systematic training, we have had success with many horses whose potential could barely be seen in the beginning. With correct work it can be surprising what results can be achieved, but so much depends on the conformation and individual characteristics of the horse (temperament, willingness and submissiveness) and the ability of the rider.

Natural gaits

Walk and canter are the gaits the horse uses most in his natural state. The wild horse walks in order to find food, and runs away from danger, when necessary, in canter. The trot is the least 'natural' of the gaits and it can be improved the most. The walk and canter must always have a 'natural' quality.

Trot

The trot should be a precise, energetic and ground-covering gait in which the horse moves his feet in equal diagonal pairs, with all four feet being raised significantly. The opposite of this is dragging the feet along the ground, which can be seen by the horse scuffing the surface with the toes of his hind feet. The horse should trot with impulsion in a clear two-beat rhythm. Impulsion contributes to the horse

An extremely good example of natural ability in trot with a soft contact and in self-carriage – Dresden Mann at the German National Championships.

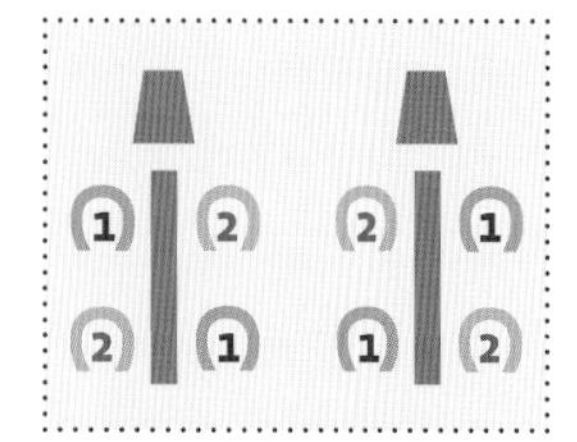

The sequence of footfalls in trot: left fore/right hind; right fore/left hind.

developing free movement of his shoulders by moving with a swinging back and with hind legs that step forwards under his body.

This gait can be improved easily with basic training. It is a simple, two-beat gait and seldom has many faults. There are four recognized variants of trot: working, collected, medium and extended.

Working and medium trot are used mainly in basic training.

In *working trot* the tempo is slightly more than the horse offers naturally. The rider maintains the energy by well-timed driving aids and encourages the horse to go forwards without increasing speed. Hopefully, this happens in most cases. There are hot-blooded horses, however, who are over-eager. With such a horse the rider must not drive him forwards but just remain quiet and maintain a calm, fluid movement. The rider asks the horse, as earlier, to step quietly forwards to achieve a big, ground-covering stride. Cavalletti work (see next chapter) can help, as can rising trot in a quiet tempo over ground-poles.

In working trot the hind feet should step into the hoofprints of the forefeet. The gait is developed in the working phase of the training session. We must first loosen up the horse properly so that he is able to work freely in a rhythm. Afterwards, he must be allowed to 'chew the reins out of the rider's hand' before having a short break in walk on

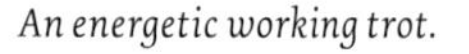

An energetic working trot.

loose reins. Then the reins are taken up again and trot work resumed. It is necessary to sit lightly in the saddle to develop the weight aids by allowing the horse to move through his back under the rider's seat. Sitting too deeply in the saddle at this stage could restrict the horse's back muscles and make him tense.

For the next phase we will concentrate on the working part of the training session. We begin to sit in the saddle a little in the first week after riding the horse for the first time. We wait until the back muscles are loose and strong enough. It is important not to introduce medium trot too early, and better to ride a few lengthened strides at the end of the session. Medium trot should be introduced into the training programme when the horse can accept the rider sitting in the saddle without tightening the back, and accept half-halts so that he can be shortened again from longer strides while remaining in an even tempo. The strength required for medium trot is developed by first collecting the trot. In the beginning, a lively working trot is sufficient for lengthening the stride.

Lengthening the stride with plenty of impulsion.

Have confidence in yourself!

Without this the trot will not develop further.

At the end of the session the stride can be lengthened in rising trot on the long side and shortened again on the short side. This exercise helps the hind legs to lift off the ground and step through with more impulsion and bigger steps.

It is important that the steps do not become hurried. If this happens, the tempo should be reduced by half-halts and the exercise started again. This should be repeated a few times to find out whether the horse has misunderstood or whether his muscles are not yet strong enough and his back not loose enough to maintain the required length of stride.

The rider must *feel* how much can be asked from the horse (for example, increasing the stride slightly on the first long side, then more on the second long side, making absolutely sure that the rhythm is maintained, and then asking for the most on the third long side). At the end of the exercise the horse should be allowed to *chew the reins out of the rider's hand*. We go onto a circle to do this using a couple of half-halts to steady the horse, before opening the hands and encouraging the horse – not forgetting to drive him forwards – to take the reins forwards and down, chewing on the bit. Every horse who has been flexing through the poll will need to stretch out his tired neck muscles.

Benchmark – chewing the reins out of the rider's hands

Being able to allow the horse to chew the reins out of the hand is the indication that his work has been correct.

The rider can be satisfied when the horse chews the reins out of the hand with his neck stretching forwards and down (not in a backward direction), and his back relaxing and loosening. Then the rider can sit and drive. If the horse comes behind the bit and does not stretch his neck forwards and down, then the training is not correct. The rider has neglected encouraging the horse to reach forwards to the bit and the horse's back remains tight. In this case, on the following day, the rider must make absolutely sure that the horse is loose in his back and is driven forwards to the bit.

(If the rider forces the horse into an incorrect outline with strong reins and has not been using the driving aids correctly, the horse may try to pull the reins from the rider's hands when invited to stretch down, or he may raise his head and gnash at the bit. These are signs of tension in the neck muscles and a result of poor riding.)

After the reins are chewed out of the rider's hand this part of the training session should be followed with a short rest in walk on a loose rein before beginning another exercise, for example, progressing to canter work.

Medium trot is a further development of lengthening the strides and works best once a degree of collection has been established. It is

'Chewing the reins out of the rider's hand' to make sure the horse is working through his back at the end of a session.

Energetic steps from behind when lengthening the stride.

recognized by impulsive, long steps ridden in a longer frame. The horse should reach out in order to cover the ground. Impulsion comes from powerful bending and stretching of the hip and stifle joints. This makes it easier for the movement to flow forwards through the swinging back and over the well-developed top line of the neck, through a flexed poll and a soft mouth to the rider's hand. The rhythm, impulsion, contact, outline, and working through the back are regulated by half-halts. True impulsion is only generated if the horse takes weight correctly on his hindquarters, with a relative elevation of the forehand. The horse's nose should be just in front of the vertical.

(The development of extended trot comes later as it demands a greater degree of rideability and collection. Logically, then, extended work is not part of the young horse's training – collected and medium trot must be established first. We will, however describe extended trot as part of the complete picture.)

Extended trot is the pinnacle of forward movement in trot. It demands the greatest possible impulsion and requires quite special co-ordination on the rider's part. The rider must be able to sit to the horse's supple, swinging back in order to ride a correct extended trot. The prerequisite for extended trot is a fully developed collected trot.

Collected trot will not yet be fully developed in the training of the young horse. For basic training we only require the beginning of

Correct training is an achievement in itself: the development of carrying power.

collection, achieved with half-halts, and this beginning of collection comes at the end of basic training. Collection requires a well-developed ability to work through the back and, the better the musculature is developed, the better the future collection will be, enabling the horse to remain in an even tempo as collected trot develops. Lofty, animated steps with lowered haunches, a shorter outline and raised neck are the distinctive characteristics of collected trot.

Canter

Canter is a jumping movement and is the quickest of the three basic gaits. The horse should canter with impulsion, covering the ground in a three-beat rhythm. The moment of suspension occurs when the horse leaves the ground with all four feet (preferably cantering 'uphill'). The opposite of this is a short, hasty stride without any expression. A ground-covering canter occurs when the horse takes big, impulsive strides with a supple back and lowered haunches, jumping forwards and upwards with plenty of spring.

The sequence of footfalls in canter is as follows:

1. outside hind
2. inside hind and outside fore
3. inside fore
4. moment of suspension.

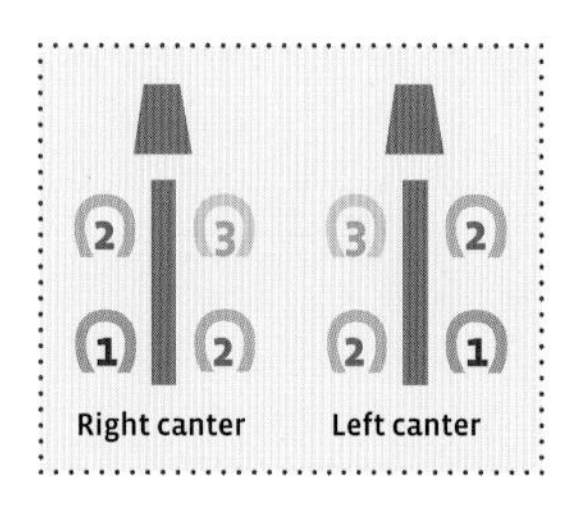

The sequence of steps in canter.

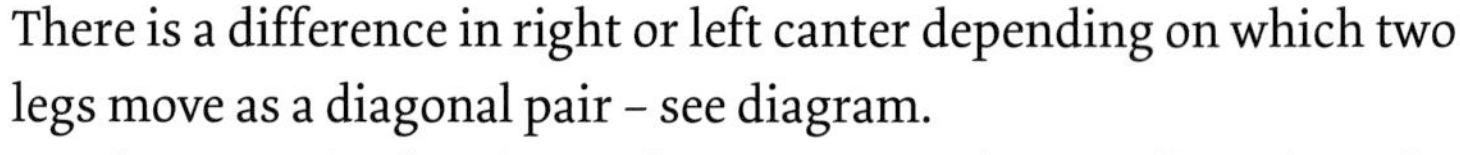

There is a difference in right or left canter depending on which two legs move as a diagonal pair – see diagram.

The recognized variants of canter are working, collected, medium and extended. If the rhythm is lost and an incorrect leg sequence occurs, this is described as a four-beat canter. An example of this incorrect sequence would be:

1. outside hind
2. inside hind
3. outside fore
4. inside fore.

A correctly ridden canter has impulsive forward steps with a clear moment of suspension. An impressive canter shows lively and

A good example of a balanced canter.

beautiful steps. Canter exercises have not been covered very much in previous chapters, as it is important first of all that the horse is obedient to the rider's aids in trot.

How do we ask for canter? We start in working trot on a large circle (initially on the horse's easier side) at one end of the school and give a half-halt on approaching the closed-in half of the circle (going towards the wall). We put our weight to the inside, moving the inside hip forwards and stepping into the inside stirrup. In the next moment, we place the outside leg behind the girth and keep the inside leg lightly against the horse. Canter is asked for with an energetic press forwards of the inside seat bone, bracing of the lower back muscles and pressing with both legs (the inside leg remains at the girth and the outside leg a hand's breadth behind), and we give forwards with the inside hand. The whole process lasts for one or two horse's lengths, or a couple of seconds.

With a young horse it is advisable, when he is not too fresh, to maintain the canter for a few times around the circle, as long as he has no difficulty balancing under the rider's weight. The canter aids must be refreshed at each stride to prevent the horse falling into trot. Once the horse has been returned to trot or walk he should be praised and given a loose rein before repeating the canter from trot on the other rein.

Transitions between trot and canter on a circle develop the canter stride.

An uphill canter stride, full of impulsion.

Transitions from trot to canter should be repeated several times on the circle before riding around the whole school and allowing big, natural strides. The fluency of the canter must be maintained by the rider's aids. We must not make a fuss if the horse canters on the wrong leg; we know the horse has a strong and a weak side and the natural crookedness of the horse will be as apparent in canter as it is in trot. The rider's inside leg must be used more to help prevent the effects of crookedness. Usually young horses find left canter easier because, through natural crookedness, it is easier for the left hind leg to take weight. This is the reason why we ask for canter on the easier rein first before asking for the more difficult one. We must make sure that we give the correct canter aids, and do not collapse at the hip.

Quiet canter work strengthens muscles.

With further training, the canter aids are fine-tuned. There will come a time when the seat aid will not be necessary in order to ask for canter. (As the horse becomes more responsive to the rider's aids, an aid with the outside leg will be sufficient to instigate a strike-off into canter with the outside hind leg. The rider's inside leg will then encourage the horse's inside hind leg to step forwards under the horse's body. The rider's back then follows the movement of the horse's back to maintain the canter without a strong seat aid being necessary.)

Long periods of canter do not help the development of the stride. The horse becomes tired and can lose impulsion. The best way to improve the canter is by frequent transitions from trot to canter on a circle. The ride should try to ask for one or two circles in trot and two to three in canter. As the horse becomes looser and more able to work through his back, the transitions can become more frequent as they improve. It is good to aim for half a circle in trot, and half a circle in canter. At this stage of training the horse is not experienced enough to collect and improve the canter with half-halts. This next, more advanced level, comes when transitions from walk to canter and vice versa are possible. This helps the hindquarters to lower and take more weight (essential when riding a course of jumps or cross-country).

When the horse is loose and can perform working canter in self-carriage, a few steps of medium canter can be asked for on the long side. The canter strides should be longer and cover more ground. The strides should not be flat, but 'uphill', with a lowered croup. It is normally only possible to ride medium canter in a dressage seat. We can, however, refresh the working canter in a light seat in the same way as riding cross-country, with the horse's neck slightly lower and with the poll flexed.

A clear picture of the inside hind foot stepping under.

A quiet canter is very useful for strengthening the back muscles. At the St Georg Riding Club, Munster, there is a canter track around the outside of the arena so that we can loosen our horses up better on straight lines. In our experience the horse's movement in trot and canter can be bigger if there is the opportunity to loosen them up and work them on long stretches of ground, such as a racetrack, at some point in the training programme. It is much easier, and common

Cantering in a light seat at the beginning or end of the session takes the rider's weight off the horse's back.

Taking the inside hand forward to pat the horse.

sense, to allow the horse freedom of movement during training. Cantering cross-country is ridden in a light seat (jumping seat) during basic training.

As a part of dressage training, extended canter is used in the same way as extended trot. However extended work comes out of collection and there is little development of the collected canter in the basic training of the young horse; as a rule it comes into the second year of training up to Elementary level. An important test of the horse's self-carriage, which can be applied in the earlier stages of collection, is to '*stroke the neck*'. This is more usually done in trot, but is also important in canter. When stroking the neck, both hands are taken forwards along the mane until they reach the middle of the neck. The contact must be released for one or two strides before the hands return to their former position and re-take the contact with the horse's mouth. Unsettled horses can be quietened down by stroking the neck. The rider's seat remains unchanged; only the hands are moved forwards from the elbows. The horse may take his nose forwards as long as the tempo, rhythm, and outline stay the same. If he does so, this is an indication that he has been trained correctly. Finally, to make sure that the horse is working correctly into the outside rein, the inside hand can be taken forward in the direction of the horse's mouth and can quietly pat his neck. This is useful when riding curved lines.

Testing self-carriage – 'stroking the neck' in canter.

Walk

The walk is a marching gait. The horse should move in a clear four-beat rhythm and cover the ground while moving fluently forwards. 'Marching' means that all four feet move up and down in a purposeful (lively but not hurried) manner. The opposite of this is a 'shuffle'. The horse covers sufficient ground in walk when the steps of the hind feet just overtrack the hoofprints of the forefeet in medium walk, the degree of overtracking being greater in extended walk.

Being in four-time, the sequence of footfalls at walk is such that it can be described in different ways. If starting from the front (with, for example, the right fore) the sequence would be: right fore, left hind, left fore, right hind, a sequence that may be described as split diagonal pairs. If starting to count from behind, the same sequence will appear as: right hind, right fore, left hind, left fore – the footfalls are first on one side, then the other. If the sequence of steps is not regular, the feet may tend towards moving in lateral pairs, in which case the horse can appear to pace. This can be seen whether one counts the footfalls from the front first, or the back. Horses who do not cover the ground often pace when collected walk is asked for.

If just one leg takes a different step from the others, then the horse is not in the correct rhythm. Any deviation from the qualities of 'marching', 'four-beat', 'fluent' and 'ground-covering' renders the walk faulty.

We can differentiate between medium walk, extended walk, and collected walk. *Medium walk* is the equivalent of 'working walk'. The horse marches fluently, evenly and without tension. The hind feet should overtrack the hoofprints of the forefeet slightly. In *extended walk* the horse takes larger steps, which are as long as his conformation allows them to be. It is most important that he does not rush. The hind feet should clearly overtrack the hoofprints of the forefeet. The rider allows the horse the freedom of his neck while keeping a slight contact

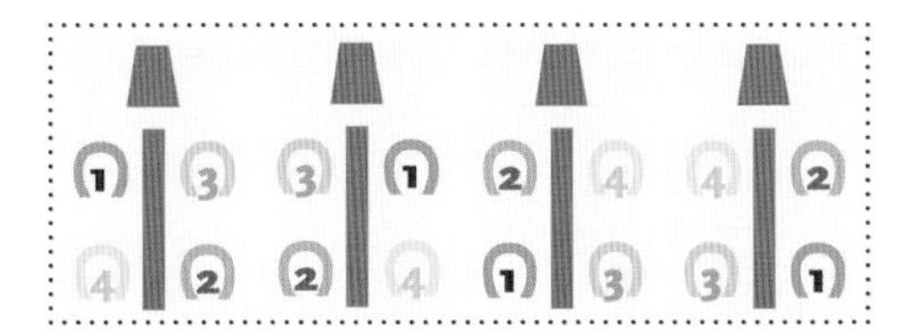

Sequence of steps in walk.

This horse is walking freely on a loose rein.

Common faults

One of the most common faults in walk is riding in walk with hands that either hold too strongly or pull back, and do not follow the movement of the horse's head and neck from the rider's elbows.

to maintain flexion at the poll. In *collected walk* the outline of the horse's neck should correspond to the amount of collection asked for. The steps are shorter than in the other forms and the hind feet should step into the prints of the forefeet. The joints of the hind legs should bend more, and it is most important that fluency and rhythm are maintained.

During basic training the walk cannot be improved very much, but it is easy to cause problems. The movement of the head and neck should not be restricted by the rider having tight elbows. It is especially important in transitions trot–walk and canter–walk to keep the elbows soft to achieve good walk steps immediately after the transition.

In our experience, young horses who have learned to work into a steady contact, flexing at the poll, in trot and canter can also do the same in walk at a later stage. We have not found it satisfactory, with our horses, to attempt to reverse this process.

Basic ground rule

Unless there are really good grounds not to do so (see text), the rider should begin in walk on a loose rein.

To develop the walk, every trainer should know the importance of ending each training session in walk on a long rein, maintaining flexion through the poll. Beginning a session on short reins straight away can disturb the rhythm which can be difficult to improve later on.

There are some situations in which one has good grounds for not starting on loose reins:

- With very young horses, for reasons of safety and to help achieve a steady contact with the bit more easily.
- When riding horses who are unsettled on loose reins at the beginning of the session and refuse to march quietly but hurry along taking short steps. (This can often be a sign of tension, or it can be caused by incorrect use of draw-reins.) These horses are better ridden on a long rein maintaining poll flexion.
- Horses who have too much muscle under the neck and a weak top line are better ridden on long (not loose) reins in order to relax the underside muscles and to encourage the top-line muscles to stretch. This is easier to do after working in trot first.
- Horses who gnash their teeth should walk on a long rein in order to loosen the neck and establish the neck carriage in order to make the first trot easier.

Requiring much feel from the rider: walking on a long rein.

In these situations the rider must remain aware of the fact that young horses in the first year of training need reins that are as long as possible, so the rider maintains a steady contact without flexing the poll.

We must also make sure that the young horse in the first year works only in medium walk and, whenever possible, on loose reins. Problems of rhythm in walk can be avoided by riding on long reins at the end of a training session without flexion at the poll, a requirement in Novice and Elementary dressage.

The effect of conformation on basic training

Conformation and possible physical defects must be taken into account when training a young horse. On the whole, one can say that the quality of horses has improved over the last 20 or 30 years of breeding. Good advice for trainers is to select ones with good conformation, but there are also ways of improving horses who are not naturally ideally built.

Good points of conformation to look out for when selecting young horses for training are:

- Well-developed hindquarters; a long, sufficiently sloping croup.
- Active hind legs.
- A normally swinging back – long enough without being too long.
- A broad back, pronounced withers and a long, sloping shoulder.
- A high enough base to the neck that is not too wide, and a neck of a good length with muscle along the top line, and not too much on the underside.
- A narrow jowl where the head is set on, giving freedom to the lower jaw when flexing.
- A long mouth.
- Reasonably flexible fetlock joints.

There are three angles in the region of the hindquarters that should be examined. These, and their desirable angulations, are:

- Hip joint/point of ischial tuber/stifle (about 90 degrees)
- Point of ischial tuber/stifle/hock (about 90 degrees)
- Stifle/hock/fetlock (about 135 degrees).

These should appear to work together easily. However, the most important angle is the slope of the croup. A flat croup can result in upright hindquarters. It is difficult to measure the angles precisely, but

With a good neck carriage, such as this, the horse should easily work with his head in front of the vertical.

An example of a compact horse with well-developed hindquarters and lovely top line.

one can assess the angles of the joints by eye and tell whether the hindquarters are in proportion and look as though they can develop impulsion and be able to take weight. Well-developed hindquarters work well in all gaits and the canter will be 'uphill'. It will be harder to build muscle if the horse has less desirable angles to his joints. However, improvement can be made through training, by riding, for example, changes within the gait in trot and canter, improving lateral suppleness by asking for wide, crossing steps, and asking for bigger steps, especially by riding extended trot. In walk the length of stride is hard to alter and in canter the strides can remain short and with less flexing of the hocks.

Active hocks allow powerful and energetic stepping forwards and under and produce trot steps that cover the ground. By contrast, straight hocks tend to produce dragging steps, which can affect later training when piaffe, passage and further lateral work are required. Slight improvement *can* be made, but the limits are set by the horse's natural conformation.

As the centre of movement during normal exercises and figures (mainly in trot and canter on a circle), the ideally conformed back loosens easily and is thus a very important requirement for training the young horse. A horse with this characteristic will be able to collect later on without becoming tight in the back. Also, once a loose back

A low-set neck which is rather short.

has been developed, the muscles are able to contract and extend easily. A loose, swinging back enables the power of the horse to transmit forwards from the hind legs, through the back, top line of the neck, poll and mouth into the rider's hand. The ability to work with a swinging back is thus of prime importance.

The other extreme is the straight, tight back that is not so easy to loosen, swings less freely and is harder to sit to. A long, weak back makes it difficult for the horse to take weight behind and a short back swings less easily. A hollow back, even with a well set-on neck, results in the horse 'pushing his back away' and raising his neck in transitions.

A long, sloping *shoulder* allows freedom of movement, particularly in extended trot. Together with this feature, pronounced withers mean that the *saddle area* is further back towards the hindquarters. Placing the weight of the rider in this area of the horse's back makes it easier for the horse to take his weight on his hindquarters, which is especially important in further training. Short, upright shoulders and flat withers limit the freedom of the shoulder (tight through the shoulder). This is most obvious in extended walk and extended trot and can cause the horse to be on his forehand, which can later lead to injuries of the forelimbs.

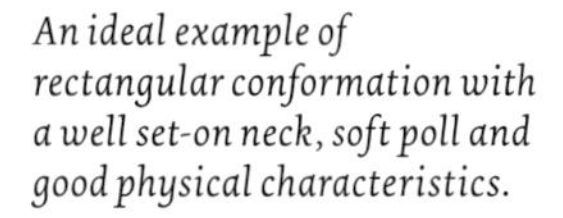

An ideal example of rectangular conformation with a well set-on neck, soft poll and good physical characteristics.

A well set-on neck should be placed high on the shoulders and be of good length. It should not be too wide, but should have a well-developed top line and not too much muscle underneath. This is important for training the young horse with regard to acceptance of the contact, working through the back and, later, collection. If the horse does not naturally have this structure, the muscles must be developed appropriately before further training can proceed.

The muscles in the first third of the neck, just in front of the withers, are very important for later acceptance of the contact, working through the back and lifting the forehand. The neck must be long enough for good balance both in dressage and for jumping (especially when taking off and landing). It is vital that the horse is allowed to use his neck to balance when riding cross-country, particularly when riding up and down hill and tackling drops and water jumps, to avoid accidents or injury.

Sleep Late

With the grey, Sleep Late (English Thoroughbred), who has a somewhat low set-on neck and straight crest, it has been posible to establish a steady and acceptable contact by using a correct length of rein and sensitive co-ordination of the aids.

Sleep Late, Saumur 2004.

It is easier to establish a soft contact and flexion at the poll with a slender *jowl*, which allows sufficient freedom for flexion of the jaw, making the horse easier to ride. Common problems can stem from either a thick jowl, narrow jowl, or a tight jaw. The space between the jaw bone and neck must be large enough to accommodate the salivary glands and the connecting muscles. If this area is too narrow, the ability to work through the back will be restricted and it will be less easy to establish a correct contact, both of which affect straightness and future collection. If this fault exists, working on a longer rein can be useful with young horses and, when jumping, a correctly fitted running martingale can be helpful. Draw-reins only cause problems, even when used when warming up, and they cause the wrong muscles to build up even more. (In our experience *draw-reins* have no place in the training of the young horse. Using them a lot causes resistance, tension, incorrect muscle building and an unhappy horse. At the Westphalian Riding and Driving School in Munster, they possessed only two martingales and no draw-reins at all and we don't use them ourselves.) Sensitive riding will always be necessary to accommodate this defect.

A narrow jowl can make it easier to flex the horse at the poll, but hard hands will cause overbending very quickly. With this conformation, soft hands and elbows are necessary to be able to give at the right

The modern Warmblood includes more Thoroughbred blood than used to be the case.

moment – not forgetting the support of the driving aids. Allowing the horse to chew the reins out of the rider's hand and stretch down also plays an important role.

A long enough *mouth* not only gives more room for the bit (both snaffle and double bridle), but also more space for the tongue to lie under the bit. To train a young horse with a small mouth requires a correctly fitting bridle with a bit that is not too low in the mouth or too thick, and a soft hand. Tongue problems are not unusual with this conformation and can cause the rider difficulty.

Long, sloping *pasterns* (but with not *too much* flexibility at the fetlock joint) affect the looseness of the back and how easy the horse is to sit to. A short, tight shoulder combined with upright, short pasterns can result in overloading of the forehand. There is not a lot a rider can do with a young horse with this conformation apart from making sure he works on soft surfaces and avoids hard, uneven ground, which could lead to injury.

Assessing the horse

Assessing the horse is not about glancing briefly at the faults, but observing the horse as a whole.

All horses have small defects in their conformation. It is the responsibility of the rider to be aware of these problems (in the back or neck, for example) when riding various exercises during the horse's training. A horse who is not perfectly built can still turn out to be a very good horse and perform well.

The effect of temperament on basic training

Training is much easier if you have a positive attitude towards the horse.

When training young horses the different characteristics of each individual, such as temperament, ability to perform, amiability and learning ability can play an important role. Through improved breeding, character faults such as kicking, biting and rearing are less common now, but these problems can still occur through poor handling and bad training.

Temperamental difficulties are less common with horses who are handled correctly – an important point for all riders, whether they ride as a hobby or professionally. It is relatively easy to recognize a fundamentally temperamental young horse and to handle him appropriately. In our experience women are more sensitive when it comes to dealing with this sort of problem, where sympathetic handling produces the best results.

Willingness and ability are two different factors in training. A young horse should be prepared to respond willingly to all demands placed upon him in the first months of training without reacting adversely and going against the rider. This is apparent especially with free-jumping, jumping small fences for the first time with a rider, and

This expression says it all: motivation, co-operation, self-confidence and trust.

A positive attitude

Things are much easier for a rider with considerable confidence whom the horse can trust. Being successful and enjoying the training process results in a happy, confident young horse.

when tackling the first ditch or water obstacle. The limits of the horse's *ability* can be seen, for example, when free-jumping, and such horses should not be overfaced. There are some young horses who are very willing, but do not have much ability. In cases such as these the rider's knowledge and experience must be applied to work carefully with the horse over a period of time.

Friendliness is shown in a young horse by his willingness to be groomed, tacked up and led in hand, allowing the rider to mount and dismount without any problem. Such a horse is a delightful partner to work with. The horse's temperament influences the behaviour of the rider and the groom, and vice versa. It is very important that the young horse enjoys being ridden, and derives pleasure from having contact with people.

Memory plays a very important role in the young horse's training, a factor that is unfortunately often overlooked. A young horse not only remembers good experiences, but also the bad ones. If, for example, a young horse is frightened in a noisy corner of the school one can halt, talk to him, and ride quietly forwards again, or ride behind another horse. Alternatively one could use the whip and spurs and ride through the corner with strong aids. In the first scenario, the next day the horse remembers being quietly ridden, spoken to calmly and rewarded, and gains confidence. The frightening experience is soon forgotten. In the second scenario, he remembers the whip, spurs and rough handling, and naps before the corner, expecting to be punished again.

The position of the ears shows how much this reward means.

The same principle applies when jumping. For example, when first attempting a water obstacle whilst cross-country schooling, following a lead horse is far better than resorting to the whip. Negotiating the obstacle and being rewarded gives the horse confidence, which is vital in basic training.

Giving him a bad experience, such as misuse of the whip or being pulled in the mouth, is the worst thing one can do to a young horse, and it doubles or trebles the resistance factor. There is no harmony established between horse and rider and the detrimental effects are considerable.

On the other hand, good, thoughtful riding in such situations is beneficial to both horse and rider, and is essential for young horses.

CHAPTER 6

Cavalletti work

How it began

Training with cavalletti, and with it the 'light seat', was developed in about 1930 in Italy. (To be precise a single raised pole is called a 'cavalletto', but this term has never been used in Germany. [*Since this correct singular form is also unfamiliar to most English speakers, the German convention has been retained – ed.*]). Graf Rothkirch, the commander of the German cavalry in Paderborn at this time, trained for a while in Pinerolo and Tor di Quinto at the Italian cavalry school. He soon realized the training possibilities for horse and rider of using both cavalletti and the light seat in basic schooling.

In the style of the Italian school, groups of riders used four cavalletti to help loosen up every day in walk and trot for about 10–15 minutes. Eight to ten young horses, at one or two horse's lengths apart, were ridden quietly in rising trot over the cavalletti. The distance between the second and third cavalletti was doubled to allow for the different length of stride of each horse. Loosening the horses' backs in this way was very beneficial and the benefits became particularly noticeable in later jumping and cross-country training.

After the war the basic principles of cavalletti training and the 'light seat' were upheld by a former Paderborn rider, Paul Stecken (the last active squadron leader of Riding Squadron 4 and successor to Baron von Nagel/Ittlingen) who later became manager of the Westphalian Riding and Driving School. The training possibilities were of great value in many lessons for both young and older horses alike. Nowadays, training of this type is not often done according to the old conventions, when eight to ten horses would work together. However, this does not affect the value of cavalletti work for the individual horse; the physical effort and strength required are substantial, but the work is highly beneficial and very rewarding.

Our own connection with this work is very strong. Reiner was introduced to cavalletti work as a student at the Westphalian Riding and Driving School and later incorporated it into the training of some of his horses. His enthusiasm for the training possibilities of cavalletti work led to the writing of the book, *Cavalletti*, and we have also mentioned the importance and value of cavalletti work in our other books.

Theory

We find that studying theory complements practical training. Many difficulties in training are overcome when one does not rely just on 'feel' as a rider but also learns theoretically what to do before embarking on training a horse.

The rider is responsible for the well-being of the horse. Only a healthy horse, whose muscles and condition are carefully monitored, can perform well over time. Horse and rider should be partners but this partnership cannot survive without the rider being ultimately responsible for it.

Medium walk on a long rein, maintaining a light contact.

Cadenced steps into a light contact.

Freiherr von Langen (dressage gold medallist at the 1928 Olympics) once said 'Have self-discipline and respect every living being.' He was an early advocate of cavalletti work, but why is it so useful for training both horse and rider and how can it best be used?

Training the horse is about improving natural gymnastic ability. The horse's all-round musculature and physical strength should be improved and the joints made more flexible; an important factor when it comes to improving the gaits and movement of the horse. Cavalletti work is invaluable as part of this training. Muscles are built and strengthened by movement. When they are not correctly worked by contraction and relaxation the wrong muscles develop, causing problems. Cavalletti work is a way to ensure controlled development of the muscles and to improve the horse's movement. The horse develops higher and more powerful steps and becomes more sure-footed. The joints of all four legs become more flexible and as a result the quality of the gaits is improved.

With dynamic contraction and extension of the various muscle groups the important muscles required by the horse for movement are strengthened. However, if cavalletti work is done for too long or the cavalletti are set too high or too far apart for the horse, his natural rhythm can be disturbed and there is a risk of muscle strain. Muscles

To make things easier as there are no wings to hand, this youngster follows a lead horse.

Helping a young horse to concentrate.

only develop correctly when their movement is in accord with the natural functioning of the related joints. Only cavalletti work that is systematic, increasing the difficulty of the exercise over time, will improve a horse's musculature. If done in this way, it is suitable for improving stiff or weak muscles, especially for horses with problems caused by bad riding. Horses with low-set necks, who tend to come behind the vertical, can be encouraged to work the correct back muscles. After a short time, they can work much better from behind, with fluid movement and a lighter forehand. The horse's back is able to swing and becomes more comfortable for the rider to sit on.

Furthermore, horses who have been ridden over fixed poles learn to be well balanced; they are more confident in their steps and can judge the length of their strides better when jumping. Balance and surefootedness are particularly necessary when riding cross-country over uneven ground.

Rising trot should be used over cavalletti with young and inexperienced horses so as not to disturb the swinging of the back and the development of the correct muscles. Cavalletti work helps one to understand and work with the mentality of the particular horse. The way the horse copes with cavalletti – whether he is quiet and willing or strong and resistant – is indicative of his temperament, character and intelligence. Different demands can be made from the horse by varying the exercises and changing the layout of the cavalletti. The horse becomes more attentive and, above all, more confident.

The important point regarding the usefulness of cavalletti work in basic training is this: *cavalletti work makes basic training easier for all horses. It offers the opportunity to overcome problems in jumping and dressage and is unsurpassed in developing a safe and natural way to ride cross-country.*

Practical equipment

Having praised the value of cavalletti work, the following equipment issues need to be mentioned.

Safety

Using plastic blocks rather than cross-ended cavalletti minimizes the risk of injury.

Poles set at various distances

The poles used should be made of wood and should be thick, round and hard so that the horse is careful about stepping on them and they will not split if hit, which could cause injury. In length they should be between 2.50 and 3.50 m. Traditionally, the supports at each end come in three different types: rectangular, square, or cross-shaped. Rectangular supports are not very secure when stood upright; cross-shaped and square ones that can be placed at three different heights are better. It is important that the cavalletti are heavy enough not to move readily. Light ones can be tipped over easily, causing injuries.

Injuries are, in fact, less likely if substantial poles set on plastic blocks are substituted for the traditional designs. For example, if a

1

2

1 *A maximum of four cavalletti should be used in sequence.*

2 *Cavalletti set at three different heights.*

young horse ran out when going through cross-ended cavalletti, he could scrape his legs or, when working on the lunge, the line could get caught over a cross-end, but these problems will not arise with plastic blocks.

Normally the lowest height of the cavalletti should be 15 cm and the middle height 25 cm, both of which are suitable for walk and trot work. For canter they should be set 40 cm high to help the horse push off from the ground at each step, and to help him concentrate.

The correct distances are:

Walk: 0.90 m approx.

Trot: 1.20–1.40 m

Canter: 3.00–3.20 m

Substitutions for cavalletti

When no cavalletti are available, poles can simply be placed on the ground. Heavy poles should be used to prevent the horse rolling them. Raising the ends of the poles onto plastic blocks or jump wings can make the horse work more efficiently. With young horses it may be advisable to raise the poles at one end only (raising alternate ends helps the horse go over the centre of each one) and to lay them out in a fan formation, or in a row.

Ground conditions

Ground conditions are often overlooked. For a horse to develop correctly, it is not only the number of cavalletti used and the duration of the exercise that are important, but also the state of the ground. Deep going can strain the horse's tendons and ligaments. Hard ground jars the joints and there is a risk of the horse tripping over. A good all-weather surface is the best to ride on, failing that, sand that is not too deep. The difference between riding on grass and sand is that sand is less slippery, especially when the ground is wet. In any case, the cavalletti must be placed on level ground with a good footing to give the horse confidence and to make sure that he does not slip.

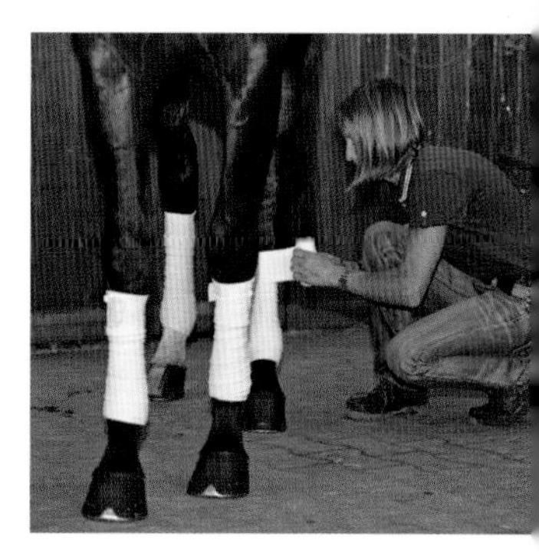

Bandages protect the horse's legs.

Equipment for the horse

The horse's legs should be protected with either boots or bandages. It is very important to protect the legs against injury from a shod hoof when stepping over cavalletti. Running side reins can be used when lungeing to encourage the horse to stretch forwards and down over the cavalletti.

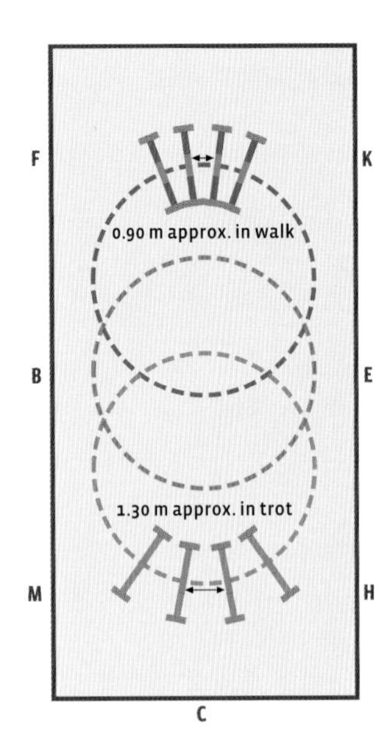

Cavalletti layout for lunge work.

On the lunge

Lungeing the horse over cavalletti can correct stiffness in the neck and improve the ability to bend through the ribs. Flexing the horse's body on a circle causes the inside muscles of the ribs and haunches to contract and the outside muscles to stretch. The inside hind leg has to step more forwards and take weight. These benefits are increased when working over cavalletti because the horse's joints have to flex more and his muscles have to work harder. The length of the steps can be altered by increasing or decreasing the size of the circle without having to change the layout of the cavalletti. The horse can be returned to a normal stride length the next time around.

One must take care that the lunge line does not get caught on the cavalletti, especially when using traditional patterns. The line of the circle must be maintained over the cavalletti, which are closer together at one end and wider at the other, so that the horse does not drift in or out. The trainer must therefore have correct lungeing technique and ensure that the horse works between the whip and lunge rein.

Positioning the cavalletti

For training on the lunge the cavalletti are best positioned as in the diagram. They do not need to be altered during exercise, and thus allow the horse to become familiar with the layout. The difficulty can be increased by adding more. It is important to space the cavalletti precisely, especially with young or inexperienced horses, and to make sure they are correctly aligned on the circle. A helper is very useful. The middle circle is used for lungeing without cavalletti. One circle is set for trot work, and the other for walk. The outsides of the cavalletti should be blocked off with jump wings or raised poles for safety reasons (especially with very young horses). If eight cavalletti are not available, six (three at each end) would be sufficient. It is very important to set them at the correct distance apart and make sure they are on the line of the circle.

Phase 1: starting lungeing without the cavalletti

Although we have referred elsewhere to using cavalletti work as part of the loosening up process, this does not mean that the horse should go

1

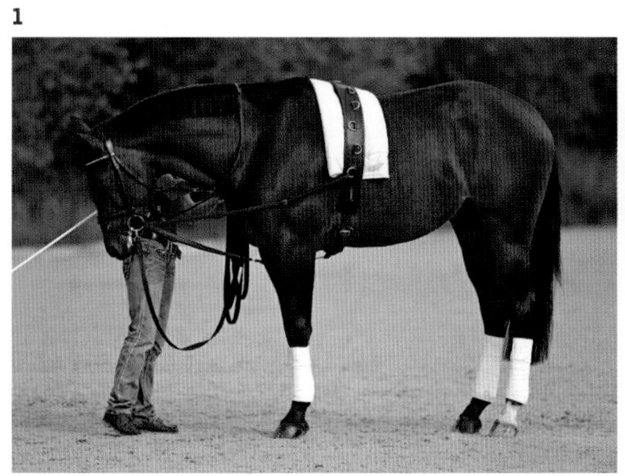

2

1 *Fitting running side reins.*

2 *A relaxed trot with running side reins.*

over cavalletti as soon as he enters the school. A few minutes loosening up on the flat must always precede cavalletti work. In this instance, the horse should be worked on the lunge with a light contact, but calm, balanced horses can be loosened up without side reins. The horse should be allowed to trot and canter on the middle circle for 5–10 minutes. Most horses are a bit fresh to start with and should be spoken to quietly to calm them down and to establish a normal tempo. Small taking and giving aids on the lunge line should be used. Sometimes a horse can be asked to work almost straight away, in which case the work phase can begin after a few circles.

Phase 2: putting on the side reins

After changing the rein and lungeing in the other direction the side reins can be put on, or shortened to give the horse a contact to work into. Generally, running side reins are simplest to use. Taking heed that the horse will be going on a circle, the inside side rein should be slightly shorter than the outside. The difference in length depends on the age and conformation of the horse (how the neck is set on) and can vary from 3 to 8 cm. The outside side rein controls the amount of bend and prevents the horse from falling out through his outside shoulder.

This equipment ensures that the horse remains safe during work. Whether the horse has a saddle or roller, the side reins should be fastened at a height corresponding to just below the saddle flaps to ensure that he can stretch forwards and down. The length of the side reins must be correct at the outset so that they do not have to be altered

A steady contact with the lunge rein guides the horse over the middle of the cavalletti..

Variety is fun

Work should never be monotonous. Taking pleasure from movement benefits the whole training regime of every horse..

during the training session. A roller is preferable to a saddle as the side reins can be fastened into the rings, avoiding the problem of them sliding down too low, as can happen with a saddle.

First, some exercises should be done on the middle circle (for example transitions trot–canter, and trot–walk). In trot and canter the horse should be asked to work with the whip and voice aids and should not be allowed to lower his neck too much and drop the contact. After about 10–15 minutes, in which work has been done on both reins, work over the cavalletti can commence.

Phase 3: lungeing over cavalletti

The young horse must first learn to be confident with cavalletti and should be allowed to go over a single one a few times in walk or trot in the first session so that he becomes accustomed to stepping over it.

Once he is confident, the additional cavalletti can be introduced in the form shown on page 132. One begins in walk and finishes with trot (maintaining a steady tempo) over the other set of cavalletti before changing the rein. With horses who are already familiar with cavalletti the complete cavalletti set-up can be used from the beginning. After lungeing the horse on the middle circle, working on a larger circle over the cavalletti increases the difficulty but, at the start of the cavalletti work, the horse must be allowed to step over the middle of the cavalletti to find his normal length of stride. Furthermore, the exercise of increasing the size of the circle should first be practised on the middle circle before it is attempted over the cavalletti.

To make the circle larger, the whip is used in the direction of the horse's shoulder. One can also step towards the horse to encourage him to move outwards. First, the exercise over the cavalletti should be done in trot, as it is easier for the inside hind foot to take more weight in this gait. The horse should be asked to go over the cavalletti five to eight times, making sure he does not become tense, before returning to the middle circle and asking the horse to move out onto a larger circle.

Changing between the middle circle and the cavalletti in walk and trot is an important part of building the correct muscles. The horse must be worked on both reins, even if he is stiff on one side. He will relax more easily by starting off on the easier rein. It is important not to go on for too long on his stiff rein and it can be useful to finish off

This horse is stretching forwards and downwards, chewing the bit, without side reins.

This horse trots happily into a light contact.

on the easier rein again for a few moments to ensure that the session ends on a good note. A young horse who has some difficulties in the beginning is often improved with four or five sessions either lunged or ridden over cavalletti.

Duration of cavalletti work

A session of 40 minutes in total is sufficient for lungeing over cavalletti, and the training should be as follows: 5–10 minutes in walk, 5–10 minutes without side reins, 5–10 minutes with side reins without cavalletti and about 10 minutes in walk and trot over the cavalletti. To finish, the horse should be allowed to walk for a few minutes without side reins so he returns calmly to his stable.

1–2 *A relaxed trot with active steps from behind, supported by a steady contact from the lunge rein.*

1

2

Riding straight over the centre of the cavalletti.

Cavalletti work under the rider on straight lines

Ridden work is the most difficult part of cavalletti exercises. Everything so far has been preparatory work for further training and lays the foundation for responding to the rider's aids in the saddle.

Different cavalletti layouts

Before every training session it is important to work out the exercises to be included and how to set out the cavalletti. There are many different cavalletti layouts that can be used for straight-line work. The simplest is to place the cavalletti in a line alongside the wall on the long side of the arena, or out in the open parallel to the track. The horse should be able to stay straight over the cavalletti without easily running out and the rider needs to prevent any tendency to do this by riding correctly. If horse and rider are both inexperienced at cavalletti work, then ground-poles should be used first. Going over cavalletti set on the inside of the track is more difficult as a correct turn must be made in order to approach them straight. To make it easier, wings can be used on each side. By way of variety, the cavalletti can be set out on the centre line of the arena, which makes it easier to change direction and to work on both reins.

Using poles as wings in the early stages of cavalletti work.

Cavalletti work in walk

Cavalletti can first be introduced under saddle when the horse is easy to ride in a straight line. One starts with a single unit and gives the horse a loose rein. The driving aids keep the horse straight. The first approach should be well prepared and the horse encouraged by the voice. The rider's upper body should be inclined slightly forward to stay with the horse just in case he jumps. If the horse steps calmly over the first one, a row of not more than four cavalletti (set at 0.8–0.9 m apart can be introduced.

It can happen that a horse will panic when he first sees a row of cavalletti, in which case it is important to take some away. Once he is settled, they can be replaced, making sure that the difficulty of the exercise is not increased too suddenly. Once the horse can cope, the final cavalletti layout can be used. The reins should be given away the first time so that the horse is free to find his balance. It is important to

1 2

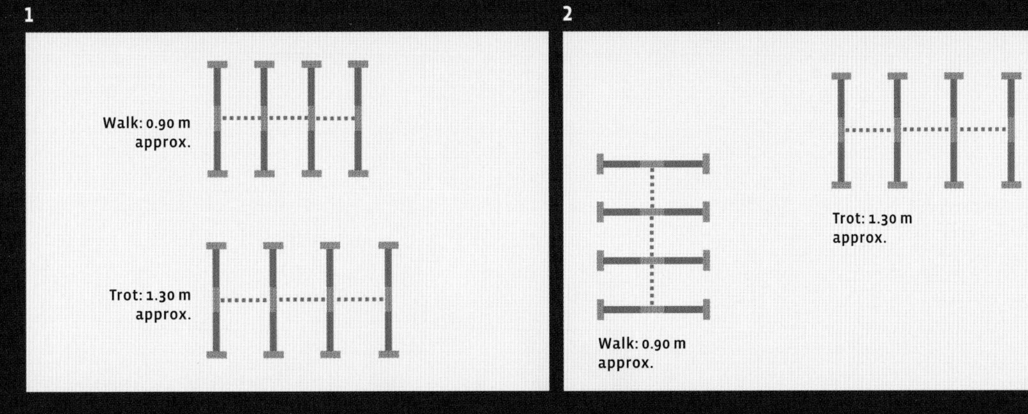

3 4

5

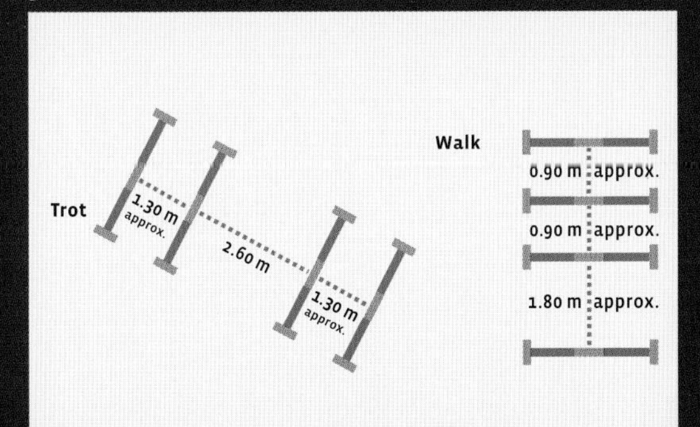

1 *Cavalletti layouts for both walk and trot on the long sides of the arena.*

2 *Cavalletti set for walk on the short side, and for trot on the long side.*

3 *Cavalletti set for walk with a stride in-between, ridden on as long a rein as possible.*

4 *Cavalletti layout for trot on the long side.*

5 *Examples of different layouts for walk and trot, with a stride in-between the cavalletti. These can be ridden on both reins.*

Riding over cavalletti with a stride in-between develops suppleness.

check that the distance between the cavalletti is suitable for the individual horse's length of stride, and they should be altered as necessary. The horse should walk over them in the natural footfall of the gait, with even steps.

Only medium walk should be used over cavalletti and it must be ridden on long reins but with a light contact with the bit. The young horse should just overtrack the hoofprints of his forefeet with his hind feet in medium walk.

The length of stride is determined by the distance between the cavalletti. To maintain regularity, the young horse is next ridden on the bit, with the weight and leg aids pushing him into a soft contact with steady hands. As soon as the horse lowers his neck and accepts the contact he can be ridden over the cavalletti. It can be helpful to keep the hands low. At about one horse's length before the cavalletti the rider's hands should give forwards in the direction of the horse's mouth so that he can stretch his neck forward and down without restriction. The rider's upper body should be slightly forward to lighten the weight in the saddle. The horse should reach down with his nose and loosen his back muscles if he is ridden correctly over the cavalletti. However, it is not always possible to keep a soft contact with the bit. Horses with a low-set neck can hold themselves tight in the back, with a stiff neck, and go against the reins. In this situation riding

The rider's tasks

1. Riding straight.
2. Maintaining a quiet but active tempo.
3. Maintaining a long, low outline with a light contact on long reins.
4. Keeping the upper body in balance with the horse, as in rising trot with the weight taken in the stirrups.

a volte or figure of eight before the cavalletti to encourage the horse to bend and soften may help him to step under. From this point, the horse is ridden straight towards the cavalletti, and immediately allowed to chew the bit and take it forwards and down. This shows the horse how to stretch his neck down and use his back muscles correctly. The horse should be rewarded each time he does well. The exercises should be repeated a few times to achieve improvement.

The distance between the cavalletti is increased by riding at them on an angle, as opposed to straight, and this can cause loss of rhythm. Careless riding causes the horse to take fast steps which do not take any weight. Suddenly dropping the contact before the cavalletti also disturbs the horse and prevents him stretching forwards to the bit. However, the opposite of this is worse – strong hands combined with a tight seat and upright position prevents the horse's back from swinging. Also, the rider should not lean back over the cavalletti in an effort to drive the horse forwards, but should use the lower legs and the voice. A short whip can be used on the shoulder if necessary. A long whip used behind the girth can be awkward when trying to give the hands forwards.

Correct placement of the cavalletti (0.8–0.9 m) can improve the medium walk, this being enhanced by allowing the horse to stretch forward and down into the reins at least by the moment he steps over the first one. Working over the cavalletti set for trot prepares the horse well for jumping and cross-country. Setting the cavalletti so as to allow the horse to take one trot stride between them helps to keep his attention and teaches him to concentrate on where he is placing his feet.

Cavalletti work in trot

Once work in walk is established, going over cavalletti in trot is not much more difficult using the layout shown. One or two should be used to start with, increasing to four. They should be set a distance of 1.20–1.30 m and at the lowest height. The rider should lean forwards slightly, taking some weight off the horse's back and into the stirrups through the thighs and knees. The hands should remain low and quiet either side of the horse's neck below the crest. The knees should be kept firm to give a secure lower leg. The stirrup leathers should be one or

Cavalletti work is great fun and motivates both horse and rider.

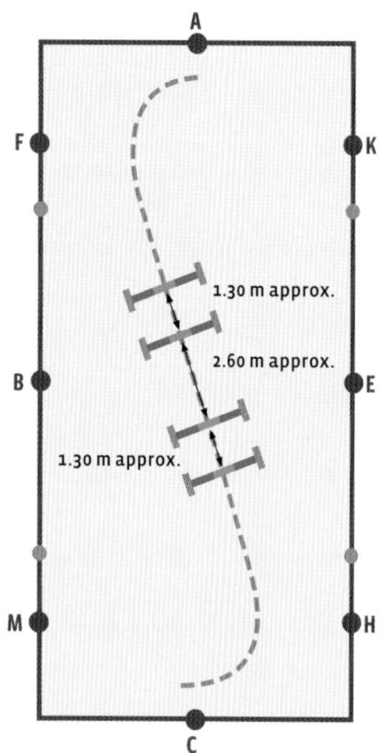

A stride in-between the cavalletti, ridden in trot.

two holes shorter than pure dressage length. Only working trot should be used when training the horse over cavalletti. In working trot the hind feet should step into the prints of the forefeet. The horse should be mentally relaxed, working powerfully forwards and in rhythm. It is important that the back swings and that the horse works from behind and without going on the forehand. The back muscles are strengthened further by the powerful diagonal steps of the trot. For this reason it is important that the horse is ridden in rising trot with a low neck. The deeper the horse stretches, the better the back muscles work.

The best exercise to loosen the back muscles over cavalletti is to allow the horse to chew the bit and take the reins forward and down.

It is fairly easy to drive lazy horses forwards. Some horses attempt to go into canter when they see cavalletti, in which case they should be put back onto the bit with half-halts and giving and taking on the reins.

If a horse goes too fast and raises his nose he becomes stiff over the cavalletti, making his back tight, and he can lose his balance. If he does not settle down after a short time, then go back to using just one. Raising the neck *slightly* is normal with young horses. However, horses with neck and jaw problems, with sensitive backs or mistrust of the bit, need to be dealt with differently. These horses need to work more

Cavalletti work develops the whole musculature of the horse: powerful steps from behind, under the horse's centre of gravity.

on accepting a contact without the cavalletti. They should be worked on circles and serpentines until they soften. When they can work deep and in a rhythm, then they can trot over the cavalletti. Further exercises such as large voltes, half-halts, or making a transition to halt before the first pole can all settle the horse before quietly attempting the cavalletti.

It is important that a quiet, even and fluent tempo is maintained before, during and after work over cavalletti. If the tempo is too fast the horse can become tense, breaking into canter or losing rhythm before the first pole. Trot work over cavalletti should follow walking over them. The whole session should last about 10–15 minutes with a short rest at some stage.

Natural beauty

Developing the natural movement of the horse (using systematic gymnastic training) makes him more beautiful and powerful.

Cavalletti work under the rider on curved lines

Once the young horse is confident with cavalletti work on straight lines he can begin the more difficult, but extremely effective, work on curved lines. Cavalletti work on curved lines is very good for improving one-sided stiffness and flexing and bending the horse equally on both reins. A horse who is not straight when riding curved lines on the flat can lose rhythm, whereas over cavalletti regular, elastic steps must be taken, with the weight taken on the hind legs. Going over cavalletti also eliminates the possibility of the hind legs escaping to the outside, since the cavalletti set the rhythm and length of stride which help the horse to maintain his natural movement.

The cavalletti should be set at equal distances in a fan formation (with some additional cavalletti placed elsewhere for loosening up work on a straight line). One should first be sure that the horse is ready to attempt this exercise, which is divided into four stages.

Cavalletti work is an important step in the basic training of the young horse.

Phase 1: loosening exercises

This first phase constitutes preparation and loosening before work over the cavalletti set on curved lines begins. About 10 minutes should be spent walking over a straight line of cavalletti on loose reins. Rising trot is then introduced, the horse being loosened by work on straight lines and curves, on both reins. Canter in a light seat on both reins should also be ridden. This is followed by cavalletti work on a straight

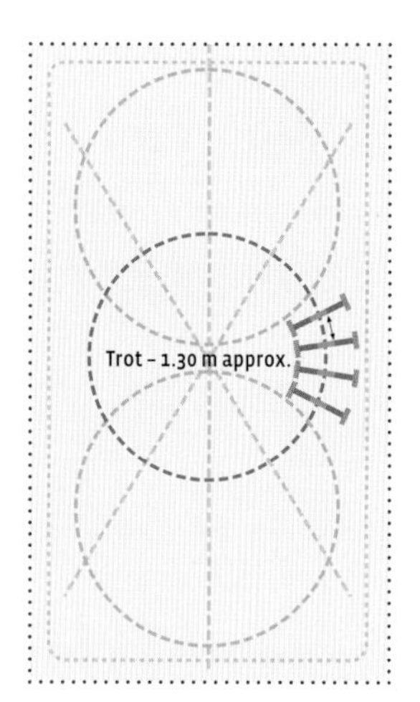

A cavalletti layout on a circle in the middle of the arena, leaving the track, the centre line and the diagonal line clear.

line in trot, the aim being to allow the horse to stretch forwards and down. After this, there should be a short rest in walk on loose reins.

Phase 2: work on curved lines

The second phase is essentially to work on curved lines. The reins should not be too long so that the rider can maintain a correct outline and feeling.

The rider takes rising trot around a circle in working trot. Shortly before the cavalletti the hands should be given slightly forward, making sure that the horse is ridden straight towards the middle of the cavalletti. If the horse is listening to the rider's aids, the same exercise can be ridden on the other rein.

If the cavalletti are set on only one circle, one can ride a change of rein 'through the circle' to change direction.

Working on the stiff side is understandably more difficult, so it is important to change direction frequently to give a horse a rest from working on the harder rein and to allow him to relax and enjoy his work on the easier rein. Transitions between trot and canter, and canter and trot help the horse to work through his back and can be ridden as follows. The rider goes over the cavalletti in rising trot, then sits and canters, cantering one circuit around past the cavalletti (on the outside) before riding a downward transition and going over them again in trot.

1–2 *Riding on curved lines improves rideability and suppleness.*

1

2

Relaxed and concentrating, working in self-carriage.

Walking over cavalletti (set at walk distance) on a straight line can also be incorporated in the work phase. The rider trots towards the cavalletti, asks for a transition to walk and rides one horse's length on a long rein before the cavalletti so he walks purposefully forwards. Another transition to trot is ridden after the cavalletti. After a few times, the walk transition can be made directly in front of the cavalletti, and the trot transition directly afterwards.

After each exercise the horse should be ridden forwards and straight, to revitalize the gait and improve the movement. Once the horse is straight, riding forwards on straight lines is always important as a means of activating the hind legs. A well-known phrase of Gustav Steinbrecht's is 'Ride the horse forwards and straight', of which every rider should take heed.

Short intervals in walk should not be forgotten. The cavalletti can be set at walk distance on a large circle. The horse should first be ridden towards the middle of the cavalletti, and then the rider should try to make the circle bigger each time round so that the distance between the cavalletti is greater and the horse must stretch more. The inside hind leg needs to step more forwards with more power and take more weight in the process.

This is almost the limit of muscle building, achieved through the horse taking weight behind. It is important to do this by increasing the size of the circle on both reins.

Phase 3: Ending the session on a good note

The third phase should ensure that the work ends gradually. The horse should be relaxed and return to his stable quietly to ensure that he starts afresh the next day in a good frame of mind. We think it is important to finish the session with an easier exercise to end on a good note and build the horse's confidence.

At the end of the work on curved lines it is worth going straight over a line of cavalletti on long reins and allowing the horse to take the reins forwards and down, chewing at the bit. In the final walk phase, the walk cavalletti can be used again.

At the end of a session, stretching forwards and downwards, chewing the reins out of the rider's hands.

Cavalletti work in canter is covered in the next chapter on jumping training.

CHAPTER 7

Jumping training

Free-jumping in the first year of training

The basic training of the young horse does not only include dressage, but also cavalletti work and cross-country riding, and especially jumping training. Free-jumping is indispensable as valuable preparatory work. Without the addition of the rider's weight the horse learns the complex sequence of movements involved and finds his own balance. There are many situations which require free-jumping such as shows and auctions, where both stallions and mares are assessed for their potential as showjumpers. (In Germany there are also competitions in free-jumping.) Intelligent people have no doubt that free-jumping is enjoyable for the horse, improves jumping technique, performance and potential and is extremely valuable preparation for jump training. The way the young horse copes is a good way of assessing his jumping ability, and to see if it is above average.

Free-jumping is also used in 'pure dressage' yards. For example Otto Lörke, a successful trainer both before and after the war, jumped his dressage horses once a week at the Gestut Vornholz in Ostenfelde.

The goals

Free-jumping brings many benefits to the first stages of jumping training.

- Developing confidence over obstacles.
- Learning to balance on landing.
- Learning to judge a stride.
- Improving co-ordination and proficiency.
- Improving concentration.
- Learning jumping technique over a fence (bascule).
- Improving dexterity.

The temperament of the young horse has a considerable influence on his jumping training. For example, crafty horses can attempt to run past an obstacle, or turn around. The trainer must be prepared for such circumstances and be quicker to react than the horse, using astute positioning and directional aids of the whip to discourage such actions.

Free-jumping requires obedience. The horse should not be allowed to use it as an excuse to misbehave and, if he does so, he should be returned to trot by the trainer. On the other hand, there are types of horse who make little effort to jump, which can happen in the growing phase when the haunches are higher than the forehand. If this is the situation it may be better to delay jumping until the horse is more physically mature. In most cases during the assessment the trainer can judge whether the horse lacks bravery or spirit (motivation).

A rather unorthodox technique, but in good balance.

Methods

With correct methods and an experienced trainer the young horse can develop further during his training by free-jumping. In practice we adhere to the following rules and standards:

- Free-jumping should be done once a week.
- Two to three helpers with whips are needed.
- Use a 20 x 40 m indoor school; with a 20 x 60 m school the horse has room to avoid the trainer.
- Mirrors should be covered, the kicking boards should be high and in good condition and the door securely closed.
- A bucket of oats, or some other treat, is needed to give rewards.
- The horse should wear brushing boots and overreach boots.
- If the horse is wearing a bridle (for leading, or to accustom him to it) the reins should be removed, or twisted and fastened securely through the throatlash.
- Use a rope without a clip to lead the horse in.
- You will need wings or a tape barrier.
- Use cavalletti (not cross-ended ones), jump stands and poles.
- A saddle should not be worn.

Useful equipment.

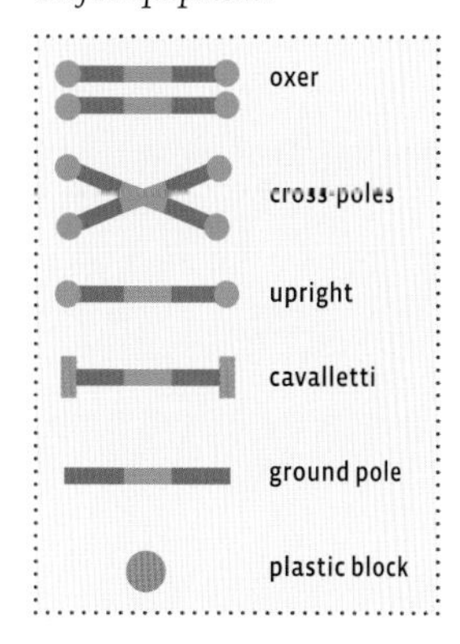

The basic obstacles (wings, or jump stands) should be positioned before the free-jumping session starts. The poles, which are added later, should be laid together to one side near the jump stands so that the horse cannot

The first experience is most important

The more carefully, quietly and reasonably one begins, the easier and less complicated future free-jumping sessions will be.

hurt himself. The stands, enclosed with wings or tape, make a passageway for the horse to go along and should reach beyond the first and last obstacles by about 3.0–5.0 m. This ensures that the horse goes straight over the first and last jumps and does not cut the corners. Any gap between the wings/jump stands and the wall must be filled with plastic blocks or other wings, so there is no risk that the young horse tries to go through it. The jumps are sited so as to be jumped towards the arena exit, making the most of the horse's natural instinct to head back to his stable. We begin on the left rein, as the horse is used to being led from this side. Looking to when the young horse later runs free it is important that he does not go too fast. In practice, a working tempo is ideal.

Before free-jumping begins, the horse should be loosened up either on the lunge or free. Usually 10 minutes are spent in walk, and a further 10 in trot/canter. This gets rid of high spirits, warms up the muscles and reduces the risk of injury. The helpers should be aware that a young horse can stop abruptly in the corners.

When free-jumping for the first time the young horse should be led in hand between the wings to familiarize him with the route he will be taking. He then can be led over a low pole positioned between the first pair of jump stands. The pole can then be raised slightly and the horse allowed to jump alone. As the jump is very low, the need to use the attraction of the exit is reduced and it should be jumped on both reins. However, nervous or strong horses should be led in walk towards the pole each time. The trainer must take special care if the horse should hesitate and must send him forwards. The second time it is necessary to be ready in case the horse pulls away or runs out.

Free-jumping on the left rein.

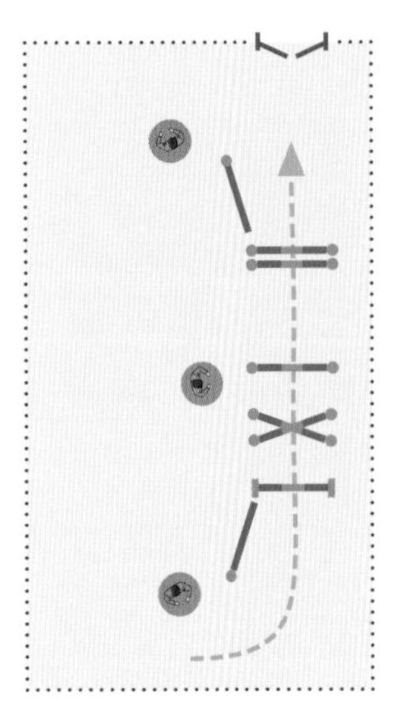

Once the horse takes the single pole happily, the number of obstacles is gradually increased. After the first pole a small cross-pole can be added, which encourages the horse to go over the middle of the jump. The next can be an upright to encourage good bascule. In total there should be three or four obstacles with distances of 3.0–3.50 m as an 'in and out' bounce at the beginning, then between 6.5–7.0 m (one non-jumping stride) to the next element and 10.0–10.5 m (two non-jumping strides) to the next. The precise length of the stride is individual to each horse, and the distance between the jumps should be altered to suit. This allows the horse to concentrate on the obstacles and not have to shorten or lengthen his stride at this early stage.

Use a simple jump for the first obstacle.

The obstacles should be between 60 cm and 1 m high. The last jump of the row should be a small ascending oxer with the back pole slightly higher than the front one to encourage fluent jumping. One helper with a whip should be at the beginning of the row of jumps, and the other at the end. The third helper remains in the middle of the school. The horse should be driven calmly forwards, but without cracking the whips. Voice aids should be used to encourage him and to praise him.

The horse must be rewarded after each successful time around and given a handful of oats or other reward in the middle of the school. This helps to build trust. While he is having a rest, the jumps can be altered.

How often and for how long the young horse should be free-jumped depends on the individual. Excitement can cause a lot of snorting and sweating, so short breaks in walk, which can be by leading in hand, are necessary. It is important to bear in mind that the young horse may not be very fit, and can quickly lose power and concentration. Free-jumping should always be ended on a good note, and the horse walked long enough so he goes back to his stable dry and calm. In the first week it is not the height of the jumps that is important, but the jumping technique.

Take care!

We have known young horses who have completed the row of jumps, turned sharply before the short side and jumped back again. This can be dangerous, for example approaching an ascending oxer in the wrong direction, and should not be allowed. If it seems likely to happen, the trainer must prevent it, moving to block the horse's line of approach and using the whip to encourage him to turn away.

Well done!

Tips for the best way of developing training

The young horse may make a clumsy attempt at the first jump as he has little co-ordination and balance. Some young horses are tense and 'cat-leap'. It takes a while for the trainer to win such a horse's trust and for him to jump more fluently.

Using five or more obstacles does not have a beneficial effect on training. The height, rather than the number of jumps, should be increased and the horse should be sufficiently confident for this after a few weeks. The jumps should be raised gradually, so as not to disturb the horse's rhythm (especially when he is cantering over the row of jumps). Making the oxer wider should be done with care.

The experienced trainer knows when a young horse has reached his limit and has had enough for one day. A talented horse will tackle higher obstacles with gusto.

While care should be taken to ensure that distances between the jumps suit the horse's stride, it can sometimes be useful to place low cavalletti between the jumps to help the horse remain in rhythm and take off at the correct place. This means, of course, that the cavalletti must be positioned carefully – for example, in a double of uprights with one non-jumping stride, exactly in the middle between the elements. If no cavalletti are available, any poles used as substitutes should be raised and secured in another way to prevent the horse rolling them.

If the horse becomes tense and unsure of himself, the jumps must be lowered. The quality of the training effect of free-jumping is dependent on routine, experience and the feel of the trainer. Care should be taken as follows:

When free-jumping, this small pony appears huge.

- At what distance and size the jumps should be set for each horse.
- Which horses are likely to canter through the jumps easily, which ones are too strong or too fast – which can go again immediately after the last jump, and which must be returned to walk first.
- Which horses jump too fast and flat over the first jump and take off too near to the last. Cavalletti or poles, placed carefully as just described, can help these horses.
- Whether the first or second jump can be raised slightly to help the horse arrive correctly at the last.
- With more talented horses the last jump can be a triple bar or a parallel.

What to do when problems arise

If the horse refuses

The jumps should be lowered and the horse brought in again and encouraged with the whip and voice. When he jumps over them fluently, they can be raised again. If a horse still continues to refuse, the number and difficulty of the jumps must be reduced.

The basics must always be re-established before continuing. The same goes if a horse has hurt himself tripping over a jump. It is important that he gets his confidence back by starting again with a low jump. A confident horse will cope with this experience better than a nervous type. The trainer must always take the character of the horse into consideration.

If the horse makes a mistake or jumps flat
Every horse can make a mistake and hit a pole. What is important is how he reacts. Most horses become more careful the next time they jump.

If a horse jumps too fast or without using his back
Horses who approach the first jump too fast can be slowed down with a bounce jump (in and out) of two cavalletti set at a distance of 3.0–3.5 m. This can be added even if the first actual 'jump' is a bounce element. Horses who jump too big over the first element (when it is not a bounce) and get too close to the next can be encouraged to jump more fluently by adding a raised pole at 3.0–3.5 m after the first jump.

In general, the training session should conclude on a good note, so that the horse views the next one positively. To ensure that this happens, it is far better to lower the jumps if the horse has some difficulty rather than to carry on regardless, and it is very important to reward the horse when he has done well, despite some small mistakes!

Our feeling about jumping young horses is that the horses will enjoy it if they are trained well, and if they enjoy it they will jump in good style.

Jumping training for young horses

Before one attempts a small jump under saddle the horse should have been trained in preparation by lungeing and riding over cavalletti and especially free-jumping. Whether one takes one, two or three months to begin jumping small obstacles depends on the individual horse and the trainer's wish. Jump training in the first year should only be done if the horse is willing. If he is, then there are certain principles that are important to follow. Training from the first jump towards coping with a novice course follows these phases:

- The first jump on the long side.
- Gymnastic jumping over cavalletti – grid training.
- Jumping single obstacles.
- Jumping related obstacles and combinations (on straight and curved lines).
- Jumping an easy novice course.

The first jump should always be tackled in an enclosed outdoor school or indoor arena just in case the horse gets out of control. The rider should always wear a riding hat and carry a short whip. It is important that only short, blunt spurs are worn. It is also important that an experienced rider jumps the horse for the first time to ensure that the rider does not get left behind and bang down in the saddle or pull the horse in the mouth.

The horse should first be warmed up and familiarized with the obstacles. He should be ridden around the jumps and allowed to sniff them, the rider praising him to win his trust. The horse should be allowed to chew the bit and stretch down in between the jumps in all gaits. The canter should be ridden in a light seat and the horse should be in self-carriage with his nose just in front of the vertical.

The first jump on the long side

As soon as the horse is loosened up and ready to work, and we can control the tempo and the direction, we start with a small jump on the long side of the arena near the wall. The first jump should be towards

A small cross-pole with wings.

An upright fence with wings and a placing pole just in front.

the arena exit, ideally following a lead horse, making things easier by using the herd instinct of the horse.

The jump could be perhaps a small cross-pole with a ground-line and should be approached in trot. When jumping towards the exit is successful, we change the rein and jump in the opposite direction away. After the jump the horse is rewarded and returned to a quiet trot with half-halts. We then do the same thing in canter. To reduce any likelihood of the horse running out, have a helper standing near the obstacle about 2–3 m away. Alternative precautions are to place an extra wing beside the jump, or to use poles either side as wings to help keep the horse straight.

If the exercise goes well the jump can be raised to a small upright of about 80 cm in height. A clear ground-line should be maintained to help the horse take off at the correct point, as the rider will not yet be able to place the horse.

The principle of this initial work is to treat the exercise as free-jumping under the rider. The rider must keep the hands low and very light, allowing the horse to look where he is going, and they must give forwards with the movement of the horse. We jump small obstacles with the young horse fairly frequently, about two to three times a week. This might be for just 5 minutes at the end of a training session, since doing it this way is less stressful for the horse. The primary aim is to build the horse's trust.

When the horse can jump fluently and without wavering over obstacles by the wall of the school, the next stage is to place a jump in the middle of the school. This should be taken a number of times, the horse being jumped quietly towards the exit. It is surprising how quickly horses learn to jump if the basic principles are adhered to.

Gymnastic jumping with cavalletti – gridwork

Once the young horse has learned to cope with single fences, gridwork can begin. A sensible lead horse, wings and jumping towards the exit all have their uses here also. The rider is always responsible for

'I know about these things already' – a confident jump over cavalletti built as a jump.

Jumping a grid improves the horse's concentration and co-ordination.

maintaining the tempo and aiming for the middle of the jump. When riding away after the last obstacle care should be taken that the young horse concentrates on the rider's aids and does not get out of control. Helpful exercises are half-halts in trot (and later transitions to walk or halt) or riding on a circle.

Gymnastic jumping demands a high level of concentration, and strength in the hindquarters, so resting frequently is important. The length of time spent riding grids varies from horse to horse. On one hand the horse learns by repetition, and on the other he can become complacent if the exercise is repeated too often. Getting the balance right requires great feel from rider and trainer, and is like walking along a tightrope.

In general, the jump stands should be put in position and the distances measured before work begins. The poles should be laid to one side by the jump stands so that only the cavalletti are used in the loosening up phase. As the training session progresses the poles are gradually raised into place. The rider should approach the grid in a light seat to avoid disturbing the horse's movement and should lean slightly forwards so as not to get left behind over the jumps. The hands are kept low and give in the direction of the horse's mouth.

The three diagrams on this and the next page show types of grid which, in my experience, are very useful to start with when training young horses.

Example 1

Example 1

Building a grid on the centre line has the advantage that it can be jumped on both reins. Begin with one to three cavalletti set so that the horse can easily trot over them. After these, place a small cross-pole followed by an ascending oxer with the poles laid on the ground at this stage. Then the jump stands are put in position for an upright and finally another oxer. Next, the rider trots over the cavalletti and the following upright, then over the cavalletti and over the oxer. To finish with the exercises are put together as follows:

trot on the left rein over the grid;

trot on the right rein over the upright;

trot on the right rein over the grid;

trot on the left rein over the oxer.

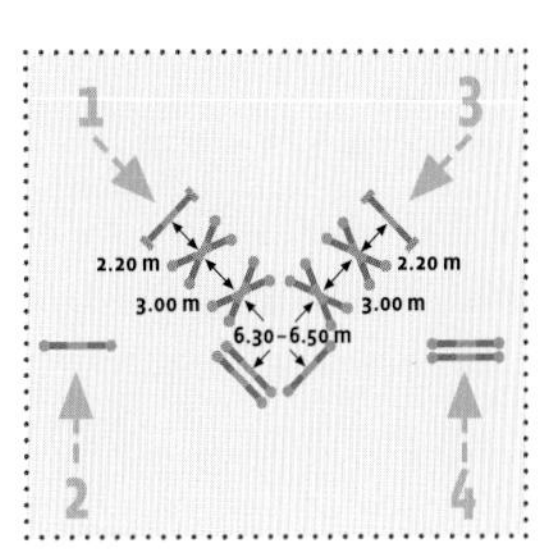

Example 2

Example 2

This example uses a trot cavalletti before the first cross-pole. The rider trots along the first diagonal and goes along the long side before approaching the second diagonal, and so on. For the next stage an upright is added to the first grid, then an oxer to the second. The rider should then allow the horse to rest while the helper builds both an upright, and an oxer, one on each long side of the school.

To finish, the separate elements are all put together. Starting on the left rein the rider turns onto the first diagonal and trots over the grid with the upright, then takes right canter and jumps the upright on the long side and returns to trot. This is followed by the second diagonal with the oxer, and the oxer on the long side is jumped out of left canter. If the young horse goes on the incorrect canter lead, he should be asked to change leg through trot.

1 *This horse trots over the cavalletti . . .*

2 *. . . jumps the cross-pole . . .*

Example 3

The grid is built progressively. It is important that the elements are built out of items that have been used before, so the horse is familiar with them. To make sure the horse comes calmly towards the cavalletti, ride towards them from a corner. If impulsion is lost, or he is lazy, ride forward on the long side in an energetic tempo and bring the horse back with half-halts on the corner.

For a young horse, I would recommend that the obstacles in the grid be no more than between 0.8–1.0 m in height.

Pushing off the hind legs builds muscle. To develop jumping technique, it is important that the neck stretches forwards and the back rounds as the horse 'bascules' over each fence. Above all, jump training must be fun and the horse should enjoy himself.

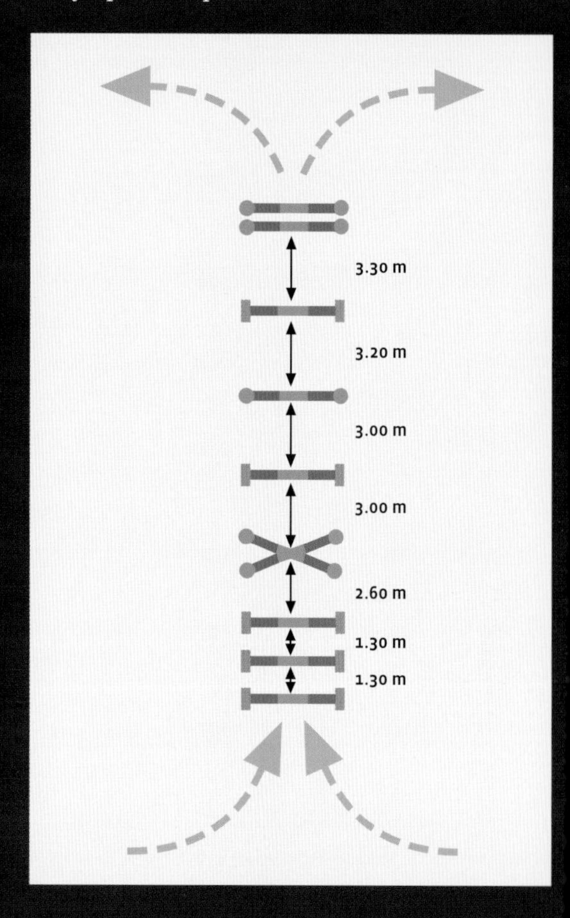

Example 3 (with cavalletti at their lowest height).

3 *. . . lands and looks at the cavalletti . . .*

4 *. . . canters over the cavalletti . . .*

5 *. . . jumps the upright . . .*

6 *. . . then lands . . .*

7 *. . . canters over the cavalletti . . .*

8 *. . . and jumps the oxer.*

Jumping single obstacles

Through gymnastic jumping the young horse has learned flexibility, how to concentrate on the next jump, and has become confident. Now is the time to jump single obstacles from canter. The jumps should be 0.8–1.0 m in height. A pole as a ground-line in front of an upright and an oxer makes it easier for the young horse to find the point of take-off. The jumps should be approachable from both sides.

The example in the diagram shows the middle jumps placed in such a way to prevent the horse from running out.

The horse is ridden once around the school to establish the canter stride and is then ridden towards the first jump in a steady canter. By riding on both reins and changing the rein the jumps can be approached in many ways. Placing a cone in each corner of the school helps the rider achieve a good line of approach with a young horse.

Jumping single obstacles.

Jumping grids and combinations

Practise riding a small section of a course at a time, making sure that you approach on a straight line for four or five canter strides before each jump. The young horse should now be familiarized with different types of obstacle. For example, there could be a wall or water tray to which the horse is introduced quietly.

New fillers need to be treated with respect!

Most riders find that young horses who are already used to gridwork have few problems with single fences of various designs. When first introducing combinations, an upright to an oxer at a distance of 7.0–7.5 m is recommended to start with in case the young horse hesitates.

Riding to a fence from a distance on a curved line is more difficult. First, the horse must be securely onto the outside aids and able to canter on curved lines. Horses who go against the inside rein tend to fall out through the outside shoulder and so jump badly over a second jump. To improve this situation, jump over cavalletti on a circle, first one on the enclosed side of a circle at one end of the school then, when that is successful, a second can be placed on the opposite side. The exercise can then be made more difficult by riding the circle in the middle of the school with the cavalletti placed on the centre line.

Jumping cavalletti on a circle – over the first cavalletti, the rider should already be looking towards the next.

Jumping a simple course

If the rider is successfully riding sections of a course, putting the elements together should be no problem. The horse should be jumping happily at home before contemplating small competitions at different venues. The horse should at least be able to canter in a controlled tempo. If he lands on the wrong leg, or is disunited after a jump, the rider should return to trot to change leg. The rider can help the horse by riding in a light seat and taking note of the following:

- Do not go too slowly (to avoid jumping too flat).
- Ride straight on the approach (to prepare the horse so he knows what he is doing).
- Aim for the middle of the jumps (to prevent running out).

It is never too early to get the young horse used to a variety of fences.

- The horse should remain in self-carriage (to keep in balance when taking off and landing).
- Be accurate when riding between jumps (to avoid taking off too early or too late, which could shake the horse's confidence).

Refusing or running out should not happen if the horse jumps with a good technique and enjoys what he is doing. Warming up properly is very important before competing: only a correctly prepared horse can do his best. When compiling a training session, the course should come at the end. Before a competition, loosening up should come first, followed by exercises to improve working through the back, and finally jumping over a practice fence. Young horses are more likely to do well if they are already familiar with the obstacles they will come across in a competition. Later on, in the second year of training, a greater variety of jumps can be introduced.

Following the basic rules, riding the route of the course and coping with different obstacles should cause no great problem. In the second year of training, a dressage rider will concentrate on dressage training and a showjumper on jump training. The basic training in the first

A perfect jump over an oxer, stylish and competent.

year is the same for all horses whether they are destined for a future in dressage, jumping or cross-country. In our experience many horses can be relaxed when training at home but may spook at unfamiliar sights and sounds at a competition, and this is something to take into consideration during the training process.

When horses become too 'strong'

We must be careful that the horse does not speed up during the course and make mistakes. These faults can be corrected by bringing the horse back sharply, but going against the rider's hand can make him even stronger. In our experience riding large, easy turns towards the jumps, using half-halts to regain balance and re-establish even canter strides works far better.

Problems and tips for solving them

Swerving out

Most horses, if they do this, swerve out to the left, as they naturally find bending to the left easier. If a young horse tends to do this, it is best to use a lead horse and have wings or poles as barriers on the obstacles.

A short jumping whip should be carried on the shoulder to the side on which he is likely to swerve out. The rider maintains a contact with the horse's mouth. Should the horse still swerve out he should be brought immediately to halt. A turn on the forehand should then be ridden in the opposite direction, the horse should be ridden back in the direction he came from and then towards the jump again.

Becoming strong

Being flight animals, it is the natural reaction of some horses to rush away. This happens particularly with hot-blooded horses. We quieten such a horse by approaching an obstacle from both reins several times. The approach should always be made from a turn. Cavalletti work and gymnastic jumping require concentration and can help a great deal in this situation. In addition to the gridwork exercises, cavalletti can be used around a single jump that the horse is rushing; one to give correct spacing before the jump, and a second, perhaps third after the jump at a distance of 3.0–3.5 m between each one. This makes the horse concentrate. In the air over the jump, the horse can already see the cavalletti as he looks down. His instinct will be to round his back. He has no time to run away and can be kept under control by the rider. If there are still problems, then a large volte can be ridden after the last pole to quieten the tempo. Finally, the horse should be returned to trot and given a short rest before beginning a new exercise. It is also very important to be patient.

A cavalletti before, and another after, an obstacle ensures a calm canter depart on landing.

Hesitation or refusal

What do we do if the horse does not approach the jump confidently? If the inexperienced horse will not follow a lead horse the exercise must be simplified. It can be best to begin again with one very low obstacle. In any case, the horse must learn to obey the rider's aids. Riding energetically forwards in canter and returning to a normal tempo can help the horse listen to the driving aids once more.

Two poles help the horse to jump straight.

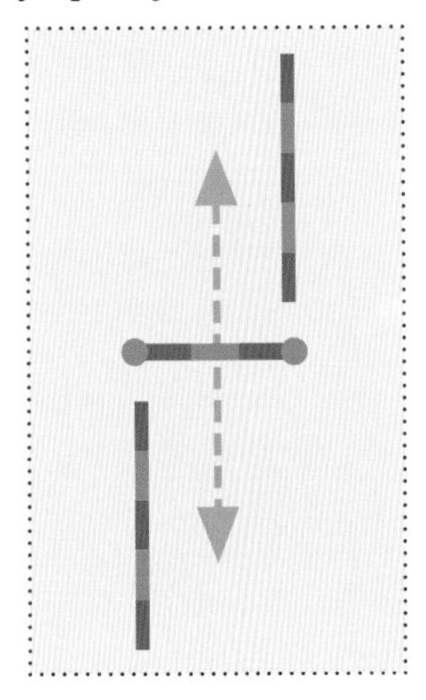

Jumping crookedly

How do we make a correction if the horse is allowed to come in crookedly, or does not jump the middle of the fence? As a correction one or two poles should be laid at right angles to the fence before and/or after it so that the horse must follow the correct line of approach. The poles must be far enough apart so that the horse does not tread on them as he lands. Following the motto 'Less is sometimes more' the rider must always take care that the young horse is not over-faced. The exercise must be made less demanding in order to keep the horse's trust. The rider must be aware that training does not always progress forwards all of the time.

With the aid of two poles, this horse jumps over the centre of the fence.

A passageway helps ensure straightness!

CHAPTER 8

Cross-country training

Getting used to the great outdoors

The basic training of the young horse should be varied and develop all his skills. Riding cross-country over varied ground and over small natural obstacles plays a very important part in this and teaches many horses to be worldly wise and sure-footed. Basically, the more the horse grows up in a natural environment and learns to work on varied terrain, the more confidently he will move. In our experience training a horse for cross-country can highlight his individual attributes, which can indicate in which direction his future lies, such as specializing in dressage or showjumping.

We will now examine the first steps of cross-county training, and continue by discussing how best one can introduce young horses to typical cross-country fences.

Even stallions can make friends while cooling off in water.

Christopher Bartle's method of 'bridging the reins'; having both reins in one hand only makes it quicker to release the reins should the horse need the freedom of his neck.

Rules

The horse should always remain securely on the aids whether in the indoor school, the outdoor arena or the open country. He must be controllable in all situations so that riding cross-country is stress-free and safe for horse and rider. However, it is not advisable to use a more severe bit to control the horse. It can easily happen that the rider gets left behind and unwittingly hangs onto the bit at the first cross-country obstacle, in which case the horse experiences pain in his mouth and can easily lose his desire to jump.

The one artificial aid that is allowed, and that can be useful with strong horses, is a running martingale. This must be adjusted long enough to give the horse the freedom to jump without being inhibited.

Before the first cross-country obstacles are attempted, the horse must have developed a good sense of balance. Also, there must be harmony between horse and rider. A naturally anxious horse needs a great deal of trust in his rider so that he does not panic and run away in unfamiliar situations. This trust requires that the rider is confident and competent. Trust requires respect and heightens obedience. The horse must respect, but not fear, the rider's aids and obey all the leg and whip aids in order for the rider to cope with all situations.

The novice cross-country rider should use a neck strap.

Equipment

For safety reasons, both horse and rider should be properly equipped. The most important item for the rider is a correctly fitting safety helmet (with a three-point harness) and a body protector. Short, blunt spurs and a whip (a maximum of 75 cm in length in total) are useful aids. Should the horse leap suddenly to one side, or make a bigger jump than expected, causing the rider to lose balance and leg position,

Be safe!

If the rider is inexperienced riding cross-country, or is a bit anxious, it can be helpful to use a stirrup leather as a neck strap. If the rider feels insecure, or loses balance, it is better to hold onto the strap rather than pull the horse in the mouth. Holding onto the mane or neck strap automatically brings the rider's upper body forward into the correct position.

there is less danger of injury with short, blunt spurs. Encouragement can be given by using the short jumping whip either on the shoulder or just behind the leg. For the latter both reins must be taken in one hand to avoid jerking the horse in the mouth. Protective boots that enclose the leg fully are important for the horse, as opposed to jumping boots that do not. Boots that protect the tendons are important on the forelegs, and those that protect the cannon bones on the hind legs. These are useful should the horse hit a fence. Overreach boots on the forelegs prevent damage to the heels with the hind shoes.

A body protector with an airbag. The safety strap is fastened to the saddle.

The demands of cross-country training, riding up and down hills and over different surfaces, make it harder work for the horse than being in the school or the jumping arena. This is why the horse must first be made fit enough, this fitness being developed by lungeing, gentle hacking and loosening exercises under saddle. This is the way to avoid over-exertion and injuries such as strains.

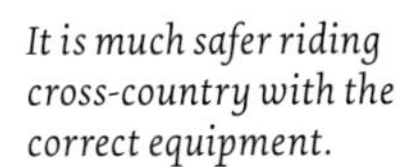

It is much safer riding cross-country with the correct equipment.

The first hack

When riding out the following rules must be adhered to:

- Always ride in a group and never alone.
- Young horses should always go out with more experienced ones.
- The order of riding depends on the individual temperament of each horse. Strong horses should go at the front of the ride.

Hacking out is fun!

- There should be a distance of two or three lengths between each horse to prevent them getting too close together.
- The horses must always be kept under control.

When one follows these basic rules, riding out is enjoyable and hacking will be fun.

Suppling exercises when you hack

Riders of young horses often ask: 'How often should I ride out and what should I practise with a young horse?' Progress through the training timetable is usually slowed down by the winter weather. Hacking out is primarily useful for loosening the horse in the first year of training. Weather and ground permitting, the young horse can be ridden out once he is accustomed to the rider's weight, to loosen him up before work, or to dry him off afterwards. Given the chance, riding the horse outside to dry off in autumn and winter is an ideal opportunity to give him some fresh air and is a good way to prevent him from getting too excitable, which can happen if he spends a lot of time indoors.

When the weather is clear, it is often cold, so a short ride in walk and rising trot in the company of a lead horse is sensible. This can last up to half an hour and can replace the training session on some days.

Most going, including asphalt, can be ridden over in walk provided it is firm enough. When training an event horse this work, which can include short spells of trot on tarmac, is essential for hardening and strengthening the tendons and ligaments. It is important that the horse is shod for this type of work.

The horse should be introduced to different ground surfaces such as sand, grass or various tracks in trot and canter where suitable. The horse should be as calm as possible and not alarmed during his introduction to the big, wild world. The more the basic dressage training has progressed, the better the horse will be in response to the rider's aids and the more obedient he will be when loosening up on a short hack. Young horses soon become accustomed to the bridleways near the school and enjoy the ride out.

Now is the time to introduce the young horse to new sights and sounds, such as open fields, tractors, stacks of wood and so on. For safety reasons he should be accompanied by an experienced horse in case he becomes afraid or tries to nap. Remember that forewarned is forearmed!

Trotting uphill is enjoyable and good for improving fitness.

We are very brave as a team!

A horse with a normal temperament calms down quickly once he has seen something new as long as the rider is not nervous and handles him confidently. It is important that the rider maintains the contact and puts the horse in a shoulder-in position (i.e. flexed away from the object) and uses the aids to prevent him from running away. This is the moment when the rider must be a tenth of a second quicker than the horse. The horse must learn to obey the rider's aids and realize that being scared is not a reason to shy or run away. From time to time the horse must have more trust in the rider than fear of unusual situations. This helps the horse to develop a more balanced temperament.

Undulating ground

Riding over undulating ground is the best way to strengthen the muscles of the horse's back and hindquarters. Depending on the level of training, this can be ridden in walk, trot or canter.

Riding up and down hills

Riding up and down hills develops strength and improves the balance, flexibility and proficiency of the horse. This work can be included in the second half-year of basic training when the ground is suitable.

Throughout his basic training the horse should remain in an even tempo, however when riding up and down hills it requires some skill in order to do this. When riding up a slope, the horse's tendency can be to slow down, so impulsion should be increased to maintain the tempo because of the extra effort required to go uphill. Some horses tend to speed up when going downhill, and so should be slowed down in order to remain in a steady rhythm.

It is very important that the rider helps the horse by sitting correctly when riding up and down hills. Uphill, the rider leans slightly forwards to give the hindquarters the freedom to push. Downhill, the rider must sit upright. When it is very steep one should ride slowly, either in walk or a quiet trot. Too much weight can be put on the forehand if the rider leans too far forwards.

When riding cross-country with several other horses it is easy to forget that the risk of over-exertion is greater, so care must be taken not too ride too hard or too fast. Horses can become excited in the company of others and will go forwards with a lot of power and often pull against the rider. Controlling this power is not such an issue in the indoor or outdoor school, but after riding out in company it is very important to check the horse over thoroughly afterwards.

Here I come! Fitness, strength and proficiency are best developed in hilly countryside.

The first natural obstacle

Once we can ride our horses safely on hacks and they trust us, we can introduce the first solid obstacle.

To succeed over the first natural jump the rider must pick a safe place with an inviting obstacle such as a small tree trunk or wood pile. It must not be too small, otherwise the horse may try to stop abruptly and jump from a standstill. The inexperienced horse may waver on the approach, so the fence should ideally be enclosed on one or both sides. This could be by a hedge, or fence, or one could use a pole or jump wing if one is available. The obstacle should be a maximum of 50–60 cm in height and preferably about 4 m wide across its face. A wide face has the effect of making the jump look lower, gives less opportunity for a run-out and, if a problem arises over the distance between the lead horse and the youngster, it allows for the possibility of both horses jumping side by side. Before approaching the jump, the rider should make sure the ground is safe (no holes and not too deep or muddy) on both the take-off and landing sides.

Alert and attentive over a small novice-level fence.

As always, before attempting this first cross-country obstacle the horse must have been loosened up – at least 10 minutes in walk, about 15 minutes in rising trot and also some canter, making frequent transitions in a light seat. It is helpful if some of this work is carried out around the obstacle, so that the horse becomes familiar with it. After that the horse should be given a long rein and allowed to blow and relax.

When first jumping the obstacle, the inexperienced horse should follow a lead horse in an energetic rising trot with two to three lengths between them. The young horse should be allowed to stretch his neck forwards slightly and look at the jump and he should not be ridden excessively deep or too strongly towards it. The rider should maintain a light contact with the horse's mouth to keep him straight and at an even tempo to prevent him unwittingly interfering with the other horse.

When he has jumped the obstacle without problems three or four times behind the lead horse, the youngster should try on his own out of trot. If he remains well under control and does not try to run off, he should then be ridden forwards in a quiet canter. If the horse becomes too strong he should approach the jump from a large circle or turn and

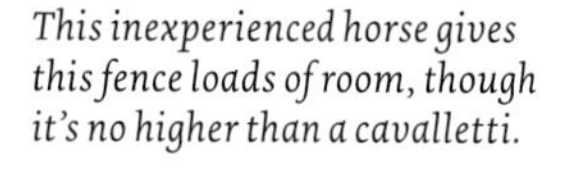

This inexperienced horse gives this fence loads of room, though it's no higher than a cavalletti.

Tempo and approach

The rider is responsible for the correct tempo and safe approach to a jump to make it easier for the young horse.

A thick tree trunk with wings is a good fence to finish with.

only be straightened three or four horse's lengths before the jump so that he sees it relatively late.

It is best to make the first jumps over solid obstacles from either a flat approach or slightly uphill. When progressing to downhill approaches the rider should be mindful that some horses jump straight but can buck or leap around afterwards. The rider must sit to remain secure in the saddle and try to keep the horse's head up so that he cannot put it between his legs. Riding forwards is the best correction for this.

Some horses back off after each jump and resist the rider's aids; this disturbs the fluency of the canter between the obstacles when progressing to more than one at a time and makes it impossible to concentrate on riding forwards. Horses who do this may benefit from more experience behind a lead horse.

Once the inexperienced horse has jumped the obstacle a few times from canter he should be given a rest in walk and allowed to relax. It is important to reward the horse after every good attempt, which gives him encouragement and builds trust.

After a successful introduction, we would then jump just two or three other obstacles in the same way. It is important not to do too

This is a bit more difficult: the fence is in shadow.

much on the first day. If this is achieved without problems, that is, without stopping or running out, a good end to the session would be to repeat the sequence of jumps three or four times out of canter. It is important to maintain a steady rhythm between the jumps. Finally, the horse should be allowed to stretch and relax in walk on a long rein.

Getting used to water

Wet areas for the dressage horse would be puddles in the arena, for the showjumper, a water jump, and for the eventer a water complex.

Second is best

You should have realized by now that it is much better to follow a lead horse. Once you feel safe, then you can try alone.

A suitable place to accustom the horse to water should fulfil the following criteria:

- The water should be no more than 20 cm deep.
- It should not have an uphill approach, as the young horse would not see it until the last moment and would be afraid.
- The underlying ground should be firm and without holes or large stones. Deep or muddy going makes the horse feel insecure and he will easily lose confidence about stepping into water.

Fear of water quickly disperses with a lot of praise and a brave lead horse.

If the horse has not so far reacted adversely to new experiences, he should have no fear of water right from the outset. The first introduction to water should be behind a brave lead horse who goes into and out of water easily and can cope with a young horse who may stop suddenly or spin around. In some circumstances it may be necessary to have the 'lead' horse beside the youngster and, if the youngster gets upset it can sometimes happen that he will slam into his companion, so the lead horse must also be able to cope with this.

How do we proceed? After loosening up, a single jump should be ridden out of trot and canter. Then use this training day to introduce the horse to other easy obstacles – it depends on the individual horse whether he is ridden alone or behind the lead horse.

A rest should be taken after about forty minutes and before introducing the water. This is not attempted at the beginning of the session because we want to ensure that the horse is quiet and not too fresh and that we have built up his confidence over other obstacles. Should there be problems going into water the horse will use his power and energy against you. He is easier to persuade if he has been ridden sufficiently beforehand and is not fresh straight out of the stable.

The first approach should be in walk, one or two horse's lengths behind the lead horse. The rider should keep a soft contact with the horse's mouth to prevent him from running out to the side. A young horse can stand quite confidently in front of a water jump, but then comes his reaction to the rider's aids.

There are two things the rider should beware of: the horse must not be allowed to turn around and, with weight and leg aids he should be prevented from stepping backwards. If he cannot be prevented at the same time from doing both, going backwards is better than turning away. This is difficult for most horses to do for more than a few lengths. Ideally, the young horse follows the lead horse into the water. If he simply refuses to move, the rider should give him a long rein and wait a moment, allowing him to snort. The lead horse should stand still in the water while the young horse is asked to go forwards again.

These youngsters already trot happily one behind the other through water.

The rider should wait for the right moment to encourage the horse to go forwards with the voice and leg aids and not suddenly use the whip, provoking resistance! If used, the whip should be applied lightly against the shoulder or behind the leg. When taking the reins in one hand, care must be taken that the horse does not spin around. After the first step towards the water the horse should be patted and reassured with the voice. If the young horse still refuses to move, the lead horse should be ridden out of the water in another direction, and then come in again beside the young horse. He should stand briefly beside the young horse and then both horses are ridden forwards together, stronger aids being used with the youngster. The lead horse should progress slowly and not get too far in front.

There is a great likelihood that the inexperienced horse will leap suddenly at the second attempt and progress with hesitant steps. If this happens, he should be praised while he remains in the water. He will snort and eventually put his nose in the water, and may also drink, in which case the rider should give the reins and wait. If he starts pawing the water and splashing, then he should immediately be ridden forwards. Holes in the bed of the water obstacle are dangerous as he could put a foot in one at this stage. Also, pawing can precede rolling, so it is best to let the lead horse come out of the water, and follow behind.

This young horse has reached the stage of cantering confidently on his own through water.

However, if the young horse has followed willingly and strides forwards without hesitation, the lead horse can remain in the water while the youngster is ridden through it. Once the young horse is out of the water, he can be ridden in again to where the lead horse is standing.

The next step is trotting into water behind the lead horse. Some horses are irritated by splashing water from the lead horse and may refuse to move. It is important that nervous horses are kept back from water spray otherwise they will not want to trot. Energetic driving aids should be used to keep them going forwards. However, the trot should generally be ridden rising to ease the horse's back, the rider only sitting when the driving aids are necessary. The next stage is to try without the lead horse.

The same steps should be repeated a few days later, going into the water at the same place before trying somewhere unfamiliar. There are some young horses who are brave and not intimidated by water. These can be taken a step further, finishing the session by cantering through the water. Some horses actually enjoy water from the beginning. This motivation should be utilized, especially in warm weather when cooling the legs in water is very welcome.

Familiarization with water is part of the basic training of the young horse and belongs in every training plan. Getting a horse used to water is not only important for the event horse: showjumpers often have to cope with mud and wet patches of ground in a course and a heavy downpour can leave large puddles in the dressage arena. Going into water is all about trust rather than anything technical. With patience and conviction your horse will lose his fear. Take sufficient time and have enough patience! Once he is confident, you can try a variety of water obstacles.

Basic rule

The challenge is not to challenge!

Jumping steps

Whether one begins by jumping up or down a step depends on what is available to you for training. For example, if your schooling area has a suitably wide ditch, you may be able to use this to jump in and out of. Another variation is a bank, which one jumps up onto first, and then down again.

Whatever you use, it is important to start with low steps. Also, the ground you will be landing on should not be too hard and should have no holes.

We prepare by loosening the horse, in this instance by trotting and cantering around between familiar obstacles, then jumping some and riding through water. If possible, it is also useful to do a little cantering up and down hills in the preparatory work. This is not only to improve balance but to exercise and strengthen the whole musculature of the horse. Trot and canter should always be ridden on long reins with flexion at the poll in a lively, but controlled tempo.

When it comes to jumping down the steps, they should be approached in walk or in a quiet trot to begin with. The rider should sit in the saddle in order to use the driving aids more efficiently. It is difficult to go with the movement of the horse in rising trot, especially if the horse jumps when the rider is rising. It is important to approach in a quiet tempo so that the inexperienced horse can jump down slowly and carefully. Be careful with young horses! They can sometimes jump down and land on all four legs together. This is one of the reasons why

1 *With sufficient freedom through the neck (with the reins bridged!), the young horse can take a good look at the steps.*

2 *The driving leg aids encourage a quiet jump down over the second step.*

3 *Landing securely with the weight in the stirrups, not on the horse's back.*

1

2

3

1

2

1 *Here, you can see how much weight the hindquarters must take . . .*

2 *. . . so the horse can jump uphill with impulsion.*

one should not jump down too high a step to start with since this can be overtaxing for the joints and affect the all-important trust.

The horse's neck should be stretched out so that he can use it to balance with as he jumps down. Even with long reins, the rider should maintain a light contact with the horse's mouth. In no circumstances should the reins be too short.

The rider's upper body must lean slightly forwards without putting too much extra weight on the forehand. Keeping the knees closed and keeping the heels down and forwards gives the rider security in the landing phase and prevents the lower leg from swinging backwards. The rider must maintain harmony with the horse by using a light seat and taking care not to land heavily on his back. The rider should sit in the saddle when riding away from the jump afterwards (at a later stage this will be out of a drop jump).

For the less experienced rider, it is always better to use a neck strap or hold the mane than to pull the horse in the mouth! Ride energetically forwards after the jump without going too fast, which can make the canter strides long and flat.

If the horse is reluctant to jump down it is important to decide whether he is not brave enough, or if he is in pain. If he has a weak back, growing problems, or undiagnosed front leg lameness, it is understandable that he does not want to jump down. If he is strong-willed, it is a matter of training and obedience. Assuming that there is no physical problem behind his reluctance it does not matter how long it takes; however, the steps should be small enough not to overtax the horse during his training.

There are horses who have no problem jumping either up or down. These are the ones with naturally good conformation, co-ordination and balance. If the horse has a weak back or poor balance, introducing him to cross-country jumps must be done in easy stages.

The next option after a step is a raised bank. With this, a lead horse is very helpful. The inexperienced horse follows the lead horse in trot, with the rider allowing the horse to look at the obstacle. (In fact, to begin with, many horses find it hard to judge exactly where to jump up. It can be helpful, before attempting to jump the bank, to stand the horse in front of it and allow him to sniff it – but the rider must take care that he does not try to jump from a standstill!)

When approaching the bank, the tempo must be lively enough to give the horse sufficient power in his hindquarters to jump up. Jumping onto a bank without impulsion can cause the horse to land on it with just his forefeet, and one or both hind legs can be grazed on the edge of the obstacle by not jumping far enough onto the bank. *When jumping up a bank, step or otherwise uphill, it is important that the rider does not get behind the movement.*

If the horse stops in front of the bank, the rider should approach again with more impulsion. Once the horse has jumped up, assuming that there is room to do so, he should be halted and praised. Once the lead horse jumps down again, the young horse should be happy to follow. With just one step down an inexperienced horse can be allowed to 'scramble down' from walk, or halt, if necessary. The bank should then be approached again without the lead horse, who should stand either on, or the other side of, the bank, but certainly not in the way of the young horse.

Riding over a small bank in canter is a good training exercise, as many horses find it easier to jump up from canter. Cantering forwards in a light seat is a way of ending the session. The horse should then be allowed to stretch down on a long rein in rising trot, and finally allowed to relax in walk and praised – a fitting end to the day's training.

New experiences should come at the end

New elements should never be tackled at the beginning of a training session. Repeat what the horse has already learned before progressing further.

Jumping down a step into water.

Jumping in and out of water

While you are introducing your horse to various cross-country obstacles the exciting experience of jumping into water should also be included. Riding your horse through water on each training session will overcome his fear, as will cooling his legs down in the water after work.

Horses who are not confident cantering through water will need to follow a lead horse when jumping into it. It is important to make sure there is enough distance between them, as one does not know how the young horse will react at first. Some make a big issue of it and leap right in, which can be dangerous for the more experienced horse who will jump more sensibly, which is why a distance of two to three lengths should be maintained at all times. If the young horse is brave, he can do it without the lead horse from the beginning.

After loosening up the horse and jumping familiar obstacles we ride quietly down a step. We also trot and canter a few times through water (somewhere that does not require a jump in) to get the horse used to the splashing.

1–2 *This young horse leaps confidently into water – the 'safety seat' should be second nature!.*

1

2

If there is an option to do so, it is best to start by jumping in a way that is not *directly* into water. For example, a small tree trunk, laid at least 4 m in front of the water's edge, gives the horse the opportunity to jump onto dry land first.

Once the horse has jumped the tree trunk and cantered fluently on into the water ahead of him, the next stage is to jump into the water over a tree trunk laid at the water's edge. The jump down should not be too deep and the whole obstacle should be small enough to be jumped from trot.

It is important to follow these steps so as not to over-face the horse. It depends on the individual whether all these stages are achieved in one session or not. New exercises should be repeated two or three times so that both you and the horse are confident. Some horses need more time than this.

Water should be approached from a steady tempo because it acts as a brake on the horse's movement. In the beginning, it is safer to approach in trot. The rider's upper body must be kept upright to help the horse keep his balance and, similarly, the reins must be given completely to allow the horse the freedom of his neck (in the same way as when jumping downhill).

Jumping over a tree trunk into water with ears pricked.

That was fun

Although the rider should not *expect* problems, it is sensible to realize that things *can* go wrong. Understanding why a problem may arise, and how best to deal with it, will help to minimize the effect on the horse. The horse could stop because he does not trust the rider, in which case he should be ridden energetically forwards behind a lead horse, or preferably be taken back a stage in training, starting again through water. Sometimes it is advisable to just canter through water a few times without a jump. If there are no more problems, then the jump can be tackled again. If the horse stops at the step and hesitates, then the rider should wait a moment, let the horse look, encourage him with the voice to take a step forwards and praise him. If an inexperienced horse stops in front of the tree trunk and will not jump down over it, the rider should start the approach again.

Only small jumps should be taken until the horse is confident and not tense any more. If the horse stumbles, he should be ridden into the water once more so that he does not become afraid.

Stairs and drop jumps

Many cross-country courses will include these obstacles. Stairs (a series of steps jumped either up- or downhill), will often include a canter stride on a flat area in between. Drop fences are obstacles which

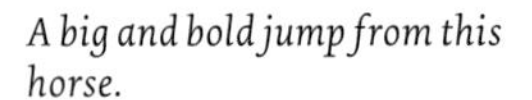

A big and bold jump from this horse.

1

2

1 *Jumping downhill requires courage and a rider with a brave heart.*

2 *The rider in a perfect seat as this young horse jumps bravely downhill.*

have a landing side significantly lower than the take-off side, and thus include stairs/steps down, and various other types of jump. With these types of obstacle one should be alert and aware of the horse's reactions.

Stairs/steps down should not be jumped from a fast tempo. It is better to slow down. This type of obstacle is a test of the rider's ability and whether the horse is responsive to the aids.

Stairs/steps up must be ridden with sufficient impulsion. The canter must be short enough for the horse to step under his centre of gravity. A long, flat canter stride that is too fast is dangerous. If the canter is too slow and lacking energy the horse will lose too much impulsion at the first step and not have enough to cope with the following one.

What do we do if things go wrong? The inexperienced horse can hesitate and stop. If this happens when jumping down, wait a moment and let the horse take a look. He should not be allowed to break away to the side or go backwards. He should be encouraged with the driving aids and the voice until he responds. The horse can jump down from halt or walk, in the same way as a single step. Make sure you reward him. The next time, as he approaches, he must be ridden forwards with sufficient energy to prevent him from hesitating again. If the inexperienced horse refuses at uphill steps, make a fresh approach behind a lead horse or ride with more determination and impulsion.

It is important that the horse remains in front of the rider's driving aids. Make sure you ride the horse forwards a few times to freshen the tempo and produce more impulsion.

When riding inexperienced horses down drop jumps one must be prepared for the unexpected. Some horses may jump too big off the top, or stumble when landing. It is important to stay in balance and not pull on the reins. The rider must have a secure and balanced seat from the outset.

Ditches

Ditches appear in almost every cross-country course. They can seem very imposing when they are deep or filled with water. It is important not to make any mistakes the first time they are included in training. The inexperienced horse needs an experienced rider. If the rider is worried, this will transfer to the horse. It is by no means unusual for the horse to stop the first time he sees a ditch. He must be encouraged with determined driving aids (and follow a lead horse until he has the confidence to go alone).

The ideal ditch for the first attempt should be dry and at the most 0.8–1.0 m wide, so that the horse can jump from a standstill if necessary. Before jumping it, make sure that the edge of the ditch is safe and visible, that is, not obscured by long grass or weeds. The horse must also be able to see the far edge of the ditch. On a cross-country course the edge of the ditch is sometimes marked with a white strip to prevent the horse from getting too close.

Following a lead horse over ditches to start with builds confidence.

Sound preparation is necessary before approaching ditches. So far, the horse has approached unfamiliar obstacles from walk. This is not advisable with ditches. Once the young horse has looked down into a ditch, he can become afraid. Also, if he does jump it from walk, he is likely to make a big effort that is hard for the rider to really sit 'with'. It is better to follow a lead horse in trot at a distance of two to three lengths; if the young horse gets too close he could tread on the heels of the lead horse if he jumps too big, in the same way as at a water jump.

The inexperienced horse should be kept into the bridle, making sure that he is concentrating on the rider's aids. The rider should sit in the saddle to make it easier to use the driving aids. It is likely that the

Brave enough to do it alone.

young horse will jump erratically the first time as he has not yet worked out how to tackle the ditch. If the lead horse is already on the other side of the ditch, the young horse may suddenly leap over. In this case it is important that the rider slips the reins and holds the mane or neck strap.

What do we do if the horse hesitates? He should not immediately be punished, but just ignored! Ride forwards energetically behind the lead horse. The driving aids must be firm enough to prevent the horse from stopping. The horse should be encouraged with the voice, either by clicking with the tongue or saying 'go on', for example. If he does

Understanding the horse's mind!

The young horse's first experiences dictate his later behaviour. If he is introduced to ditches carefully, he will learn to trust the rider on each occasion. Timid horses need more time, quiet riding and a variety of exercises. Self-confident horses must understand from the outset that they should jump when the rider asks and not take control. However this should not occur if they have learned to be obedient to the rider's aids. But if the rider has lost patience and made a big issue out of a situation then the horse will never be keen on ditches, and will perhaps remember a bad experience for life.

not react to the driving aids, then the whip should be used on the shoulder, or failing that, behind the leg. It is important to ride forwards again! This is the only way to prevent the horse from refusing.

Think about education and obedience. Once the horse is over the ditch, return immediately to trot or walk, praise him straight away with your voice and pat him, to reassure him. After a spell of relaxation in walk, repeat the exercise, using the lead horse until the young horse can jump the ditch without problems.

If the positioning of the ditch allows it, rather than refusing, the horse may run out to the side. In this case, before approaching again, hold the whip on the side to which he ran out. To put the horse on the aids, ride dressage exercises such as transitions from trot to halt and trot to canter, rein-back, changes of gait within the canter, etc. until he is listening again.

Most horses try to run out to the same side each time. Placing a wing on this side is useful, but it may be better to enclose the ditch on both sides. Follow the lead horse, and do not give the youngster the chance to run out!

Once the inexperienced horse has jumped the ditch confidently a few times without the lead horse, he should be ridden in walk and

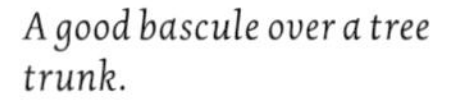

A good bascule over a tree trunk.

praised a lot. One should finish on a good note. A few days later ride in the same way over the same ditch again before attempting a new one.

Showing good style over a wall.

Other obstacles

Trakehner

A ditch with a tree trunk over it is called a Trakehner. The tree trunk is positioned over the centre of the ditch, which should be wide enough to be visible on each side of the tree trunk. The inexperienced horse and rider should be well capable of jumping the full width of the obstacle before attempting it.

Coffin

A coffin is a combination of three elements: a jump in, a ditch, and a jump out. The jump in is usually a tree trunk or another solid obstacle. The horse cannot see what lies beyond it. After one or two canter strides downhill, he has to jump an open ditch which is sometimes filled with water. It is often easier for the inexperienced horse if the ditch has a jump over the top. After the ditch come one or two canter strides uphill and then out over a second tree trunk or similar obstacle. The difficulty of the coffin lies in the depth of the ditch and how steeply the ground slopes when riding in and out.

The horse must already be confident jumping over ditches before starting with an easy coffin. If the inexperienced horse previously had problems with ditches, then he should follow the lead horse again. It is important not to over-face him. The elements of the coffin must not be too far apart, otherwise the horse may run out.

This type of obstacle requires good co-ordination and quick reactions from both horse and rider.

A confident jump over a hedge.

Hedges

Hedges are found on the cross-country course both in their natural form and as 'bullfinches' (high hedges with straggly tops which are brushed through) and 'brush fences' (artificial hedges). Jumps of a type similar to the last form were also used until recently on the steeple-chase section that was a phase of advanced events. Young horses who are not familiar with hedges of various types often jump too big over

1–3 *A triple combination with one non-jumping stride in-between.*

4 *Jumping on an angle is a regular occurrence.*

them because of lack of confidence so, when they are first introduced to hedges, these should be fairly small.

Combinations

A cross-country course includes combinations as well as single fences, the same as in showjumping. The distances between obstacles can vary, but they are always placed fairly and with a certain number of strides in between. A lot depends on the skill and concentration of horse and rider. One can practise combinations by using portable jumps such as hurdles, straw bales, logs, etc.

When you jump these as combinations, just as with single elements they should be approached fluently in an even rhythm. When jumping three elements they can each be of a different type such as an upright or a spread. The ground conditions are an important factor and should be taken into account when setting out the jumps.

Once you have practised different obstacles at home the next stage is to enter your first competition; the aim of achieving harmony and confidence over cross-country fences has been achieved. With every competition, the practising beforehand can be reduced as the horse gains experience. Establishing trust throughout the training makes it easy to overcome any doubt when riding in a competition. Trust is built by progressing in easy stages, using simple exercises. This is how you achieve your goal!

Narrow fences like this one are found on every intermediate-level course.

CHAPTER 9

Preparing for the first competition

Tips for the first competition

The test of correct basic training is the first one-day event competition. At home the familiarity of the indoor school, outdoor arena and local countryside plays an important role. The horse is not distracted, is calm and therefore easier to ride. Sometimes the rider gets it wrong, especially in the dressage phase. With the showjumping and the cross-country phases the courses are similar to those practised at home. You can lose in the dressage competition because of self-deception if you think the horse is better than he really is, and the judge's opinion can sometimes bring you down to earth with a bump. However, the judge's opinion is of great importance and notice should be taken of it. A large number of experienced judges are needed theses days to cope with the

It is very satisfying to end the show season at the National Championships.

The more experienced the rider, the quicker the young horse grows in confidence.

number of shows, classes and competitors. Basically one must trust that in every competition the judge will be diligent and judge fairly.

Every experienced rider will confess to sometimes being foolish and having been taken unawares at the first competition. Success in this situation can only come with hindsight.

At every competition one must be prepared for things not to go as planned. This applies especially with the young horse. The atmosphere at a show is unfamiliar. People, banners, loudspeakers, and many different horses all contribute to unsettling the young horse. It takes about one show season for the youngster to perform as well at a competition as he does at home. Only then can one prepare properly for each outing.

The young horse needs frequent outings to a variety of different shows before the first proper one-day event. We also load up the horses and take them to another stable yard and practice different exercises in new surroundings.

It is best to plan which competition to enter within a set timescale. Once you have planned the date of the competition, you will have a clearer idea of the necessary training programme to follow. Most horses will need to warmed up for about 30–40 minutes. A horse who carries himself easily will need less, and an excitable horse will need longer. Warming up should include loosening exercises followed by dressage movements to ensure accuracy. For the dressage phase, parts of the test can be practised to make sure that the horse understands them. It is best not to practise the whole test in case the horse starts to anticipate the movements, which can cause problems.

It is a natural tendency for the rider to want to practise the more difficult movements but this is not wise on the day of the competition. There is a risk of the horse going against the rider and becoming tense and then not performing well in the actual test. In this situation the rider and trainer have to work on tactful riding. If the horse finds certain movements difficult when working in, the rider must be careful not to spoil everything that has already been achieved in training. Just before the competition is not the time to teach the horse anything new. The rider must keep focused on the fundamentals of training, such as working through the back and keeping the horse calm in the dressage or showjumping arena.

In our experience the time allowed for *warming up* before the first competition should not be too short. Failure in the dressage test is usually because the rider has not taken long enough to warm up. It is better to take longer so that there is no pressure of time and the horse can relax. Just before the test, some lengthening and shortening of the strides should be ridden to make sure that the horse is responsive to the driving aids. Just before the start, the rider should practise the entry to the test, and praise the horse.

When warming up for the *showjumping* you could first trot over a small cross-pole after loosening up. With some horses it helps to lay a pole on the ground before it.

After the first jump the horse should be returned to trot and the exercise repeated a few times. To finish, canter a few times over a small upright, which is raised gradually. Follow this with a small oxer with the back pole a little higher. It is important not to jump too high or too many times in order to maintain the horse's trust and not tire him out.

For the *cross-country* phase the horse should cantered in a good rhythm after loosening up. Begin over a small natural fence which should be situated in the warm-up arena. Once this has been jumped

A calm, square halt whilst saluting. This should be learned as early as possible.

In harmony: concentration and accuracy – this is how it should be done!

calmly and confidently, then other obstacles can be jumped. The last warm-up fence should be jumped at competition speed.

Coping with competition atmosphere

At home one can practise 'competition riding'. The atmosphere on the day, though, is somewhat different, being unpredictable and more unsettling. This is what makes competing exciting. If one can calculate what will happen beforehand, then there is no enjoyment anymore. At the first competition, about 10–15 minutes longer than normal should be allowed for working in. We have had horses who were so distracted at first that we had to warm them up for a long time before they would pay attention. A few weeks later they were completely different and needed much less time.

Warming up for the jumping and cross-country phases should be done in a jumping seat and be ridden in the same way as at home. It is essential to walk the course on foot beforehand and plan exactly the route to take from start to finish.

With young horses the inspection of the course is very important if one is to achieve good results. At every jump the exact take-off point must be noted, and this depends on a number of factors including:

- The precise direction/line you are approaching from.
- The direction you are going in afterwards.

- The condition of the ground on the points of take-off and landing.
- The structure of the obstacles. (With combinations, this includes measuring the distance between elements and deciding at what tempo to ride them.)

The experienced rider calculates each turn in the course and the best approach to each jump.

Reflecting and learning

If there is little success at the first competition, you should not hang your head in shame. We console ourselves with the thought that young horses are not always successful at the beginning and require painstaking preparation beforehand. A horse is not a machine. Working out what went well and what did not is part of assessing

A good bascule with great foreleg technique.

Every competition is a new learning curve – even at top level.

whether the day was successful. Riders should not just blame themselves regardless, without taking these factors into account.

Every competition should be reflected upon. Questions will arise after each individual performance, indicating what is necessary in future training. This can be, for example, how to improve looseness, contact, working through the back, or correcting flexion. Every competition is valuable and worthwhile when the horse has made progress in his training and improved from the last time out. The rider gains valuable experience and knowledge from each outing which can put to good use in training. The rider can work quietly at home on improving the horse's performance.

Postscript

Personally, I train all my horses for eventing, that is to say they can compete in dressage, showjumping and almost always cross-country. I have learned this from my father, whose most successful horse, Ahlerich, jumped in his first years of training.

Also I jumped cross-country between competitions with my Grand Prix horse, Nector. This added variety to his training and was a key to his success.

The relationship between horse and rider depends on having respect for and trust in each other, and then you can, like my father and me, find great enjoyment in training young horses.

My special thanks go to Maj.a.D. Paul Stecken and my husband Andreas for their patience and tireless support.

I love riding!

Appendix

Training plan from basic training to the first competition

The following training plan has been put together as a guide for training the young horse as a riding horse and covers training through the various stages up to Novice level. The basic rules of training should be followed throughout. It is up to the rider/trainer to decide on the timescale of progress. A longer period may have to be allowed for each stage, depending on the development of the horse. Care must be taken if training is progressing at a greater speed. If it goes too quickly, the horse can suffer from mental or physical problems. In this situation an experienced trainer would recommend taking short breaks to ensure that the training stays on schedule, taking time to establish each stage by repetition and allowing time for short breaks in between.

First month (September)

Main aim *familiarizing the young horse to his new surroundings in the stable and preparing him for being ridden.*
Getting the horse used to the stable routine and change of feed and learning to trust his groom under the supervision of the yard manager. The horse is observed when free-schooling. In the second week he is introduced to saddle and bridle. He is taken for walks and gets to know the indoor and outdoor school and the surrounding area. In the second and third weeks he is led in hand. In the fourth week he is free-jumped for the first time over a small obstacle, later two or three in a row. Daily turnout in the paddock is very important!

Leading the horse is a good way to get to know each other.

To start with, canter work should be ridden in a light seat. For security, hold onto the neck strap.

Second month (October)

Main aim *lungeing and riding for the first time.*
The horse is lunged over a period of 8–10 days. Training progresses with free-schooling in the indoor school with long side reins. The horse is lunged quietly in walk over cavalletti and led over single coloured poles. In the second week he is worked on the lunge after loosening up, in a rhythmical working trot. The side reins are detached when going over poles in walk.

In the third week the horse is ridden for the first time.

In the third and fourth week we practise mounting and dismounting and familiarize the horse with the rider's weight. The presence of an old lead horse can often prevent unexpected and unpleasant experiences. Free-jumping can add variety and the enjoyment of freedom can help the looseness of the horse.

Third month (November)

Main aim *developing looseness under the rider; developing pushing power and contact on the lunge.*
Quiet work in rising trot on both reins, both on the circle and going large around the school, trot–walk transitions, stretching and chewing the reins out of the rider's hand. When possible following a lead horse in walk and trot over cavalletti and single poles. Hacking out in walk behind a lead horse – enjoying the countryside.

Introducing the driving aids of the voice and whip on the lunge. Short spells of canter on the lunge. Increasing the tempo in trot to develop pushing power and the contact with the bit, making sure that the horse does not come behind the vertical. The side reins must not be too short. Cavalletti work on the lunge is a good gymnastic exercise and strengthens the back muscles. Free-jumping; free-schooling in the indoor school – with correct equipment!

Every training session starts with a relaxed walk on a loose rein.

Fourth month (December)

Main aim *developing the forward-driving weight and leg aids; developing impulsion under the rider by lengthening the strides; the first jumping exercises.*

Introducing the driving leg aids. Riding the horse gently into the bridle and improving the acceptance of the contact under the rider (head always on or in front of the vertical). Hacking out in walk, weather permitting. Cantering in a light seat with a soft contact, ideally on a racetrack. Trotting over small obstacles/cavalletti in the indoor or outdoor school.

Fifth month (January)

Main aim *introducing the lateral aids: gymnastic jumping with cavalletti (grids).*

Loosening the horse in a long and low outline with a flexed poll and allowing him to chew the reins down out of the rider's hand several

Gridwork improves co-ordination and concentration.

times during each session. Practising turns on the forehand, leg-yielding, smaller and larger squares. Developing the halt. Further development of pushing power and security of the contact by lengthening the strides from working trot on the long side.

Cantering in the first corner of the short side and round the whole arena before returning to trot. Transitions on a circle from trot to canter and to trot again after one or two circuits.

Hacking out, weather permitting, and getting used to varying ground and water.

Continuing with lungeing, free-jumping, cavalletti work under the rider in walk and trot. Gymnastic jumping over grids.

The young horse should be introduced to a variety of fillers early on in his training.

Sixth month (February)

Main aim *riding on curved lines; jumping a variety of obstacles, riding quietly cross-country.*
Concentrating on riding through corners in the training sessions. Practising accurate circles, serpentines, large voltes, 'half-circle and back to the track' and, at the end of the month, a figure of eight on the short side to bend the horse equally in both directions, finishing with lengthening the strides. Using exercises to improve impulsion and security of the contact.

Similarly, turns, loops and serpentines can be ridden between the jumps. Developing jumping technique over single fences.

Improving fitness and condition by riding out, ground and weather permitting.

Seventh month (March)

Main aim *exercises to improve working through the back, jumping combinations and related fences: the first cross-country jump.*
In this month exercises are used to further improve reaction to the driving aids by increasing and decreasing the tempo. Working through the back 'from the rear end to the front' (lengthening the steps) in trot on straight lines and in canter, mainly on a circle. Introducing rein-back.

Hacking out is fun and is good for mental relaxation.

In the third and fourth week ride some Novice dressage tests.

Consolidate everything learned in the previous months.

Jumping related fences and combinations on straight lines. Improving the horse's jumping style over different obstacles. Small fences cross-country can be introduced.

A calm jump into water is a sign of how self-confident the young horse is.

Eighth month (April)

Main aim *to improve straightness and impulsion; riding a simple novice showjumping course; cross-country obstacles.*
Correcting natural crookedness with exercises and movements by riding on curved lines (circles, serpentines and shallow loops) and leg-yielding, with good crossing of legs on the open section of the circle in walk and trot.

Lengthening the strides and returning to working gait.

Allowing the horse to stretch and chew the reins down out of the rider's hand; 'stroking the horse's neck' in trot and canter.

It being spring (in the Northern Hemisphere), cross-country training takes priority. Practise typical cross-country fences such as water, steps and ditches, and practise small sections of a course. Riding out quietly in the fresh air is also very important.

Ninth month (May)

Main aim *the first competition.*
Going to the first competition – either a Novice-level dressage test, or a showjumping competition. Depending on the results, planning the second outing.

Tenth month (June) to end of competition season

Main aim *consolidating the training and gaining competition experience.*
Not more than two competitions with two or three classes per month. Practising specific movements required in Novice-level dressage tests. Working quietly on any problems in between the competitions and improving confidence. Do not work on anything new. Especially talented horses with an experienced rider can start working at Elementary-level dressage in a snaffle bridle (counter-canter, simple changes in canter, turns on the haunches, and 'half-voltes and back to the track') and by the end of the season compete at this level. The same principle applies to talented jumping horses by the end of the season. Cross-country training should remain at basic level, with the first competition in late summer.

Featured riders and horses

An unbeatable team: Andreas Busacker, Marie Meyer, Ingrid Klimke, Carmen Thiemann and Glen Grant, a 5-year-old Trakehner by Buddenbrock.

Zilia D, 7-year-old Holstein mare by Corland.

Dresden Mann, 6-year-old Westfalian by Dresemann.

Parmenides, 6-year-old Trakehner by Sir Chamberlain.

Hale Bob, 6-year-old Oldenburg by Helikron xx.

Franziskus, 6-year-old Westfalian by Fidertanz.

Rubinja, 6-year-old Hanoverian mare by Rubin-Royal.

Königssee, 4 year-old Trakehner by Interconti.

Llanero, 5-year-old Hanoverian by Limonit.

Spinoza, 5-year-old Westfalian by Show Star.

Diamond Rex, 5-year-old Oldenburg by Dr Doolittle with Michael Klimke.

Weisse Düne, 5-year-old Holstein mare by Clarimo.

Sir Schiwago, 4-year-old Bayern by Sir Donnerhall.

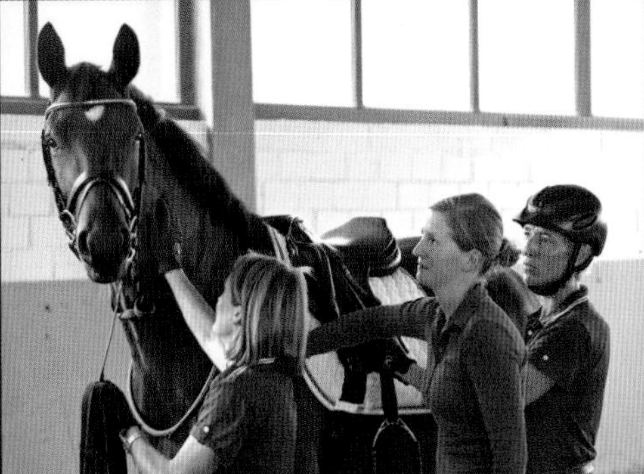

Just Paul, 3 year-old Oldenburg by Just Perfect with Carmen Thiemann, Sophie Leube and Ingrid Klimke.

Geraldine, 6-year-old Rheinländer mare by Fürst Grandios.

Sissy, 4 year-old Hanoverian mare by San Remo

The photo shoot team: Carmen Thiemann, Sophie Leube and Alexandra Haungs.

Index

Also available

This handbook describes how to work with cavalletti on the lunge, provides valuable new schooling ideas and inspiration for dressage work, as well as numerous layouts for gymnastic jumping.

Over the years *Cavalletti* has become a standard reference book. This revised edition has new photos and has been updated and extended.